Garrett,
  We really ap—
partnership + friendship over
the past 10 years!
  We're proud to be WITH
you on the trail.

        $P > E_1$

    Blquist + Bloom

Praise for *Perseverance > Endurance*

"Supremely entertaining and brilliantly practical. Two former Army special operators translate their extraordinary experiences into invaluable lessons for leadership and life. They can't make your journey easier, but their hard-earned wisdom will make you better prepared for it."
—General Stanley McChrystal, CEO and Chairman, The McChrystal Group, and *New York Times* Bestselling Author, *Team of Teams*

"*Perseverance > Endurance* is a must-read for leaders at every level. Blayne and Brandon served our country with honor and distinction, leading soldiers under the most challenging of circumstances in Afghanistan and Iraq. They've brought hard-earned lessons from the battlefield to help organizations build a culture that thrives during periods of adversity."
—Don Faul, CEO, CrossFit

"Life is defined by the moments that matter. The difference between those of us who rise up to meet those moments and those of us who falter all too often comes down to perseverance. This book serves as the definitive guide for anyone, of any age, in any profession, to persevere and conquer those moments."
—Jake Wood, CEO, Groundswell; Cofounder and Executive Chairman, Team Rubicon; and Author, *Once a Warrior*

"Blayne and Brandon's shared experiences—marked by both triumphs and setbacks—provide a compelling road map for leaders navigating adversity. This is an essential read for those dedicated to leading with strength and resolve."
—Ann Terry, CEO, Special District Association of Colorado, and Chairman of the National Coalition of Special Districts

"Without mission and purpose, we're all lost. This book is a great and honest story of what it means to have it and lose it, and find it again in service to others, even when that service looks very different—as it must. I'm proud of Blayne and Brandon for sharing their stories like this, and turning it into lessons that are useful for any and all of us who want to be better parents, teammates, and leaders."
—Jason McCarthy, Founder and CEO, GORUCK

"I have been blessed to have Brandon and Blayne in my life for many years. To say I was their leader is an overstatement. This book, built on their experiences, continues to be an opportunity to learn from them. Change is now an everyday opportunity that we all can learn from, prepare for, and execute better for our teams and our businesses. This book is an opportunity for all of us to lead better."
—Michele Zwickl, Senior Vice President, Core Lab Solutions, Siemens Healthineers

"The best leaders are both students and practitioners. Blayne and Brandon have been forged in the crucible of combat. Theirs are stories of perseverance and leadership through adversity and challenge. I am grateful for their generosity in sharing their hard-earned wisdom. All leaders—at all levels—will benefit tremendously from this book."

—Seth Bodnar, President, University of Montana

"No one is better suited to write a book about leadership than a former Army Ranger and Green Beret; Brandon and Blayne prove that in spades in *Perseverance > Endurance*. Leaning on decades of combined experience in both the military and corporate America, they beautifully illustrate principles that will make you both a better leader and a better person. From helpful charts to easy-to-understand analogies that don't get bogged down in military jargon, this book belongs on the desk of any business leader or entrepreneur who wants to be better tomorrow than they were yesterday."

—Marty Skovlund Jr., Vice President of Social Media Content
& Strategy, Black Rifle Coffee Co., and Author, *Send Me*

"Sometimes raw, always honest. Brandon and Blayne call upon their military service and corporate experiences to lay out a simple yet highly insightful way to traverse these challenges while emerging as a more elevated version of your-self. Whether you are at the beginning or end of your professional journey, the lessons and principles in this book are easily digested, which is why this book should always be within arm's reach."

—Jason Sak, Country Manager, North America,
ThermoFisher Scientific Protein Diagnostics Division

"We live in a world of rapid change, and *Perseverance > Endurance* gives us the tools to rise to the occasion. Told through Brandon and Blayne's lived experi-ences, *Perseverance > Endurance* offers an innovative perspective on leadership with a dose of humility—real, raw at times, authentic, and actionable. This book offers human-first, actionable steps to help teams persevere, regardless of your industry. I think this is a book that I'll need to read and read again."

—Sarah Roberts, Chief of Staff, Customer Success and Insights, LinkedIn

"In my decade of knowing Blayne Smith and Brandon Young, they have proven themselves time and time again to be exemplary leaders, thinkers, and storytell-ers. *Perseverance > Endurance* weaves their lived experiences (especially from their years in Special Operations) and empirical evidence to share insights on how to persevere through adversity. Their approach unpacks the difference between per-severance and endurance—with lessons and plenty of take-home tips to apply to your business and personal life. This is a great addition to any library."

—Caroline Angel, PhD, Principal, Reintegrative Health Initiative, and
Adjunct Professor, University of Pennsylvania School of Nursing

"Powerful, insightful, and deeply resonant . . . *Perseverance > Endurance* distills the essence of grit and growth in the face of life's toughest challenges. This book won't calm the leadership waters, but it will help you navigate with confidence and purpose."

—Jared Lyon, President and CEO, Student Veterans of America

"If leaders are going to take their companies to the next level, they must be clear-eyed and confident about their circumstances and their ability to change them for the better. To that end, The Ridgeline of Adversity is the first and final say!"

—Will Cunningham, Author, *Magnet Ass and the Stone-Cold Truck Hunters*

"These are two of the highest-caliber people I know, and they live what they espouse in their leadership guidance. They've invested the time and energy to understand leadership and provide invaluable, hard-earned insights for leaders facing various adverse situations and circumstances. Whether you're a CEO or first-time leader, the principles in this book will help you seize opportunities and problem-solve more effectively."

—Todd Alton, CEO, Public Trust Advisors

PERSEVERANCE > ENDURANCE

LEAD with Resilience.

GROW Through Adversity.

WIN Together.

BLAYNE SMITH and BRANDON YOUNG

Matt Holt Books
An Imprint of BenBella Books, Inc.
Dallas, TX

Matt Holt is an imprint of BenBella Books, Inc.
8080 N. Central Expressway
Suite 1700
Dallas, TX 75206
benbellabooks.com
Send feedback to feedback@benbellabooks.com

BenBella and *Matt Holt* are federally registered trademarks.

Printed in the United States of America
10 9 8 7 6 5 4 3 2 1

Library of Congress Control Number: 2024033925
ISBN 9781637746271 (hardcover)
ISBN 9781637746288 (electronic)

Editing by Lydia Choi
Copyediting by James Fraleigh
Proofreading by Cheryl Beacham and Natalie Roth
Text design and composition by PerfecType, Nashville, TN
Cover design by Brigid Pearson
Printed by Sheridan MI

Special discounts for bulk sales are available. Please contact bulkorders@benbellabooks.com.

For our families and for our teammates—both here and gone.
Your perseverance inspires us, and we strive to make you proud.
Blayne & Brandon

CONTENTS

PREFACE

So, no kidding, there we were, sipping some seriously strong coffee at a Tampa bodega after 48 hours of whiteboards, big ideas, and practical thoughts about starting a leadership development company. *We have to do this*, we thought.

It was January 2020, 10 years after we first met in Orlando at a national sales meeting, where we felt like fish out of water in our suits and ties. We'd figured out how to sell, win, and lead in this new environment, but we could sense in each other that we were built for something different. Still, we'd embraced the shock of dealing with angry clients, constant rejection, and the long, lonely miles to learn how to be businesspeople. But we had marched hard miles before.

In 1997, we entered the US Army, Blayne through West Point and Brandon through Ft. Benning's* Sand Hill. Over the next 12 years, we endured brutal training, honed our craft, led soldiers, and deployed to combat. A lot. Brandon as a Ranger in the 75th Ranger Regiment and Blayne as a Green Beret in the 3rd Special Forces Group. We experienced the full range and depth of the human experience—love, anger,

---

* Renamed Ft. Moore in 2023.

brotherhood, fear, exhilaration, guilt, fulfillment, and profound loss. We achieved great victories, witnessed astonishing scenes, and survived harrowing moments, all forever etched in our memories.

We exited service around the same time, hoping to turn the page and live "normal" lives. We took corporate jobs and did our best to adapt and make a living while quietly struggling through the adversity of post-service reintegration. On the home front, we were trying to hold together families ravaged by war, separation, and loss. We made so many mistakes, but we kept marching. We translated our combat leadership into business leadership and learned through our victories and defeats. From 2010 to 2020, we led teams; generated more than $200 million in revenue for the companies we represented; built strategic partnerships with the likes of Nike, Walmart, Microsoft, Starbucks, and Amazon; and grew a small veteran-serving nonprofit to become one of the most respected in the country, operating in 212 locations with more than 150,000 members. All the while, we built and rebuilt families and served our communities.

By January 2020, we felt gravity pulling us back together, and we couldn't shake the idea of starting a leadership development company. Truth be told, we'd tried to talk each other out of founding a leadership consulting firm for a decade, and it just didn't stick. We started Applied Leadership Partners in March 2020, just days before the COVID-19 pandemic shut down the world. With no way to meet new prospective partners and three commitments canceled, we did what we do best: *we persevered through adversity, and we led people through uncertainty.*

In the summer of 2020, MZ, the vice president of a $250 million commercial division of a global medical diagnostics company, reached out to us. Her division included sales, operations, marketing, and finance functions, with five hundred employees operating across the United States. Like most of us, the 66 high-performing leaders in MZ's division were experiencing the early signs of prolonged adversity in their business: frustration, failed objectives, disengagement, and rumors. They needed help, and by Q4 of 2020, we'd suited up and joined the team, adjusting to the virtual field of play. Throughout the pandemic, we stayed with this leadership team and brought a steadying presence by relaying principles and frameworks for leading teams through adversity.

The results were profound, as MZ shares: "You have changed how we lead and behave as a team. You made us better. We ended 2021 with record growth and didn't slow down well into the summer of 2022. Thank you! Our entire team, especially our front-line leaders, owe you a debt of gratitude. You walked us through the dark days of COVID-19, and we came out better because of you!" We remain with MZ and her team as we navigate the post-COVID-19 world.

JL, another client of ours, assumed responsibility in the summer of 2021 for the business development team of a large insurance provider covering the southeastern United States. Change always brings challenges, even when it is healthy; moreover, leadership changes surface an array of necessary adjustments and undercover resistance. JL brought us in to help his team establish a common leadership language, to launch a clear and compelling brand message rooted in their mission, and to conduct our Applied Value Creation business development training—a program birthed from our experience.

Though the challenges of change are common, every team is unique because teams are the sum total of their people, and all people are uniquely valuable. After we worked with JL's team for the past few years, its performance has improved while its retention has been steady. JL reflects upon our work together: "You are not going to find very many people who could walk in here and do what Blayne and Brandon do. Their ability to engage the whole team, guide the discussion, listen thoughtfully, and then distill down concepts into something clear and concise is unheard of and helps us out significantly. This investment was thoroughly worth it!"

Yet another client, TA, became the president of a financial firm with more than $7 billion in assets under management at the beginning of 2021. The firm emplaced this leadership change after a capital event while navigating the uncertainty of COVID-19 and market fluctuations. As the company evolved in the market, TA sought support and advice to increase his effectiveness, strengthen organizational culture, and navigate ongoing marketplace uncertainty. Through weekly coaching calls with the senior executive team and quarterly topical leadership development sessions with the larger leadership group, we have helped the team embrace the opportunity to grow during significant change and challenges.

Throughout this period of growth, TA's firm lost a critical senior leader to a new opportunity, creating more uncertainty. However, they used this transition to springboard into a new era for the company even as they kept growing. We have remained with them as they constituted a new senior leadership team from within the organization, spread empowerment throughout the firm, focused on key objectives that lead to overall success, and increased the company's resilience. TA shares, "In the last few years, we took the company from 0.5 to 3× its EBITDA, exited employees who were long seen as inhibitors of growth and obstructors of effectiveness, and retained all employees who have been critical to the company while buying up on talent."

Leadership is hard, especially if you care. But it doesn't have to be lonely. This book is about becoming the leader that a situation calls us to be by persevering through adversity. We have distilled the key concepts for leading with resilience and leading teams to achieve their next big victory. The book sums up the hard-earned wisdom we've gained from more than 25 years of leading teams through some of the most challenging and austere circumstances on the planet.

We will share with you the same principles and frameworks that helped MZ, JL, and TA forge more effective teams through their crucibles—the same principles we share with the thousands of leaders we serve every year. We know you will find it useful for your journey today. And we know you are on the precipice of your next great victory. We're here to help see you through it.

We are with you.

Blayne and Brandon, 2024

INTRODUCTION
Perseverance Is Greater Than Endurance

BLAYNE SMITH AND BRANDON YOUNG

T hough close cousins, perseverance and endurance are not the same. To successfully lead teams in uncertain times, leaders must understand and embrace how they differ to increase their ability to persevere through adversity. To help you do this, let's start by parsing out the important (though sometimes subtle) differences between perseverance and endurance.

> *Endurance is exerting the effort required to overcome a defined period of hardship.*
> *Perseverance is transforming to achieve amid continuous and unpredictable adversity.*

Endurance is admirable and valuable—critical to success because we must all dig deep at one point or another to push through hardship. We register for endurance sports because we want to know we can overcome hardship. We want to press our limits and see what we find on the other side—to know that we can do far more than our minds tell us. Thus, we have a slew of endurance sports that occupy our fitness and recreation aims: marathons, obstacle course races, century rides, triathlons, GORUCKs,* and so on. Yet there are no perseverance sports, because we're all already registered for the great perseverance sport called Life.

Life is not a series of marathons, where the distances are daunting but known. Rather, life is fraught with uncertainty. Life has checkpoints and stages but no clear mile markers or aid stations. Sometimes in life, we don't even get the T-shirt, even though we've run the race to the best of our abilities. Endurance sports give us clearly defined distances, courses, fueling stations, and yes, even T-shirts that say we did it. However, when it comes to life and leadership, there are no real finish lines. So while there will be times when we must lean on endurance, far more often life requires perseverance.

If moments of hardship require endurance, the true adversity brought about by change and uncertainty requires perseverance. Adversity results from hardships that compound in uncertain times for an unknown duration. And while hardship is the event that challenges us, adversity is the course that transforms us. Hardship is singular in this effect. Adversity is plural. Hardship is predictable and present. Adversity is unpredictable and always imminent. Whereas endurance manifests as a refusal to give way amid a particular hardship, perseverance requires us to give way *in the right direction* amid

---

* To learn about the team-building GORUCK Challenge, please visit https://www.goruck.com/pages/the-goruck-challenge.

2

adversity. Endurance requires us to hold on. Perseverance invites us to move on.

Consider it this way. With endurance, as we move from point A to point B, by the time we get to point B we are essentially a more tired version of ourselves. Not so with perseverance. By the time we get to point B, we are different from the people who started at point A. We have transformed to overcome adversity. We have grown. The experience has forever changed us. Perseverance forces us to become the person or the team that the situation requires us to be, even when we don't want to!

Because we do not typically go from one hardship in life straight into the next, we cannot train and prepare for the continuous challenges of life with a marathon mindset. We may engage certain hardships with endurance, but we cannot go from marathon to marathon because our lives are truly more analogous to walking a great ridgeline (a connected string of mountaintops) with all its peaks and valleys. To live and lead well, we must persevere when there is no marked course, whenever the ups and downs hit us, and when we are scared that we aren't enough. This is why we wrote this book.

We illustrate the difference between perseverance and endurance this way.

This book is all about persevering in the face of adversity. It is about the long game. It is about fixing our gaze on the horizon, even when the terrain before us is intimidating. And since this can be a bit abstract, we offer a framework for perseverance to give you something to hold on to. It's a place to start from, regardless of where you are within an organization or wherever your organization is at the time.

Perseverance is marked by five factors: change, uncertainty, acceptance, choice, and growth. We will explore these in greater detail throughout the book, but to make sure everything is clear, let's view perseverance and its valiant cousin, endurance, through each of the five factors:

1. **Change:** *Factors outside of our control change fast and often.* With endurance, changes are difficult but predictable. Expectations are generally met; we get what we signed up for. With perseverance, changes are difficult and unpredictable. Perseverance occurs when we're faced with the shit that wasn't in the brochure. The reality turns out to be far worse, or at least much different, than expected.

2. **Uncertainty:** *We are confronted with situations beyond our training or capabilities.* With endurance, we're shaken but confident. We feel the difficulty of the situation, but we know we can make it. In perseverance, our confidence is shaken. We aren't sure we will make it. We question our abilities and skills, and feel unsettled. Fear is the defining emotion of uncertainty.

3. **Acceptance:** *Accept the consequences, embrace the reality of the situation, and surrender what we cannot control.* With endurance, we plan for the expected and have no sense of or concern for the unknown. In perseverance, however, we do consider the

4

unknown. We must hope for the best but prepare for the worst. We are confronted by our limitations and lack of control. We don't have to like it, but we must accept it.

4. **Choice:** *Choose to become your creeds, values, and ethos and become the person the team and the situation call for.* Endurance requires us to solve practical problems with skills-based solutions. Perseverance calls us to solve novel problems with character-based solutions. Choice is the decisive point of perseverance, where we decide if we are truly willing to face adversity and grow to meet it.

5. **Growth:** *We will emerge on the other side changed; we may not feel whole immediately, but we will be better, wiser leaders, ready for the next big challenge.* Endurance challenges us. Perseverance changes us. We don't get to choose the time when destiny calls us into who we are created to be. We just get to choose whether or not to answer when it does. The fire will refine us, and we will be stronger for it, recognizing that growth may take time and reflection.

Leaders who persevere through adversity forge stronger teams, execute bold strategies, and win regardless of the challenges. They bounce back from setbacks and bring their teams along with them, refusing to fold in the face of fear. Perseverance is greater than endurance.

To begin our exploration of perseverance, we must take you back to a time when we—as young leaders—were steeped in the necessity and superiority of perseverance over endurance.

We must return to formative days that transformed our character.

We must return to times and pains best forgotten.

We must return to the war.

1

Winter Strike 2003

BRANDON YOUNG

PART I: THE KANTIWA VALLEY

4:30 AM. The alarm breaks the pitter-pattering of one more rainy Washington morning. After another long night, I leave Kelly and our baby curled up in bed. Ranger School tests you with sleep deprivation and starvation. It prepares you to lead men with your best when they are at their worst. It does not prepare you to lead a family.

The scant moments I'm home feel like "baby phase" of Ranger School, an additional opportunity to renew my leadership capabilities under sleep deprivation and exhaustion. I'm confident I'm getting a NO-GO rating, but Kel is gaining full marks. The only grader on this patrol is in my head; he is a relentless scorekeeper. His voice sounds like my father's. He is a bastard and a liar.

At least some things Rangering has taught me are beneficial in the home. Weaving my way silently through the maze of moving boxes scattered about the floor in the predawn blackness is effortless.

It is October 2003. The last couple of years have been chaotic enough for us to seek reprieve from the Global War on Terrorism and grab a chance to connect as a young family. We are hopeful for the break, with orders to Ft. Benning, Georgia, and a chance for me to be an Assessment and Selection instructor at the 75th Ranger Regiment headquarters. We've earned it. Stalking through the cardboard jungle, I softly kiss Kel good-bye on the way out the door.

I drive on autopilot. Old Nisqually Road rests under a canopy of dripping evergreens. I barely notice the turns as my breath sends wisps of fog across the cold car. It feels good to head to work in comfort. The last few years have taught me that moments of comfort are hard to come by as a Ranger in a world at war. Moments like car doors abating the rain, roads being thoughtless pathways, and dinner cooked by a beautiful woman you call yours. I'm off to work for the day, hopeful to hit the beer light early for the boys and get steak on the grill by 5:30. I'm hopeful we can get to bed early tonight too. Hopeful the baby will sleep. Hopeful that Kel and I can have some mommy–daddy time. Hopeful to wake up tomorrow without pain and the need for a pot of coffee to get me to lunch. But hope is not a strategy.

I went to work that rainy October morning and came home in December.

I am a Squad Leader in 1st Platoon (PLT), Charlie Company (Co.), 2nd Battalion, 75th Ranger Regiment. We're known as the "Madslashers," a legendary name earned by our predecessors in the 1980s—the storied Army Rangers, famed since the 1700s for suicide missions. The country expects its Special Operators to conduct direct-action raids and special missions in politically unstable environments at a moment's notice. Our business is to close with and destroy the enemies of our country, and we are the best in the business. At this point, I've been deployed to Afghanistan twice, Jordan once, and various training missions in between since the towers fell just two years prior. Those years have been a blur, highlighted by seasons of pain and tiny moments of joy: becoming a husband, a father, and a combat leader.

When the towers fell on 9/11, Kelly and I were engaged to be married that December—two kids who met one night in a bar the weekend before Valentine's Day in 2000. By the summer of 2001, we had decided to build a life together. We never imagined that life would be marked by death and war. Kelly's mother, Judy, broke the news that summer that her cancer had returned. When Kelly was a baby, Judy had ocular melanoma that took her eye but left her with twenty years to raise two kids with her husband, Lou. They were heroes to us. Lou was especially a hero to me, having lost my father at 11 to his addictions to women, money, and anything he could do to score either.

While recovering from chemotherapy, Judy watched the towers fall from her hospital bed at St. Pete's in Olympia. September 11, 2001, was her 53rd and final birthday. Six days later, on September 17, she had a day of clarity while in hospice care. Kelly and I called a justice of the peace over and married in the living room. Judy died two days later. Eight days after that, I was in Jordan for a preplanned training event that had turned into a potential forward staging area for the invasion of Afghanistan. Our sister Battalion, 3/75, would take that honor while we bitterly watched CNN from a tent on the outskirts of Amman. How foolish we were. Like kids wanting ice cream, having no idea our tummies would be sick before long.

Thirty days into the trip to Jordan, I called Kelly from a morale phone for the first time. "I'm pregnant," she said. The news hung in the tent with the desert dust. Eight months later, Jaden Jude was born in Seattle while I listened over a satellite phone in Bagram. Being absent at his birth was a blow to the soul that the scorekeeper refused to let me live down. Missing it was a choice that I covered with a lie for 15 years. I chose the war. I would be damned if I was going to miss leading my Rangers in combat. But that was not something a man could explain to his new bride.

I made it home in July 2002, just a few weeks after Jaden's birth. Bitter and ashamed, I drove on. Right on to Ft. Benning for NCO school. The day after Christmas 2002, we deployed back to Afghanistan and got stuck there while the war in Iraq kicked off in March 2003. The lost company of Rangers, C Co. 2/75 plus 3rd PLT (Earth Pigs) A Co. 2/75, remained in Afghanistan while the rest of the Regiment took it to Saddam with the big Army. We made it home again by the summer, figuring we might get some reprieve until our next rotation in 2004. We figured wrong. C Co. 2/75 spent most of 2003 in Afghanistan, and the powers that be decided that we (and the rest of the 75th Ranger Regiment) would return to finish off the winter.

War in JSOC* is a bitch that way.

My Company's First Sergeant, 1SG G., reminded me of this in no uncertain terms when the balloon went up that October morning in 2003. A mountain of a man, 1SG G. had just moved to Washington from Georgia as I was trying to move to Georgia from Washington.

---

* Joint Special Operations Command.

In a few words, he confronted me with the cold truth of the Ranger life when the country called.

"You're coming."

Pleading with him was fruitless, though I tried my best to explain the problem that leaving would cause my family. The movers were scheduled and the house was half-packed with a sale pending.

"Figure it out. My wife is figuring out how to unpack a home on her own. Your wife is figuring out how to pack yours."

It was hard to argue that point standing at parade rest in his new office—new, with bare walls. No matter how high in the food chain you are, there's always someone higher. Candidly, this was not a man ever to argue with. Though he was new to the 2nd Ranger Battalion, he was a well-known Ranger from the 3rd Ranger Battalion who had jumped in the initial invasion. So he immediately had our respect. And he had a new company to take to war that needed all of its squad leaders, especially one of its senior leaders. As the Weapons Squad Leader, I was the third-highest ranking man in the 40-man platoon (behind the Platoon Sergeant and the Platoon Leader) and responsible for the platoon's most casualty-producing weapons: three M240B medium machine guns. I was also the company master explosives breacher. When you're a young Ranger, you pray to be deemed "mission critical" someday. The title loses its luster when you're an absentee husband and father.

Arriving at Bagram was always an interesting game of I Spy—a new shower trailer here, a new gym clamshell there. Sometimes, you'd get a jeep marked up by the previous battalion with words like "Hate Train" written on it that would feel like a love letter from a friend. I'd giggle and know that my buddy John from 1/75 was here. We'd gone to the Ranger Indoctrination Program (R.I.P.),* Ranger School, and NCO school together, and he was a model Ranger leader. Other times, you'd return to find the "Hate Train" in a heap, blown up, beat up, or broken down in the mountains. The once reliable vehicle that carried us on long, dark roads was destroyed—no longer trustworthy. No news on John meant that he went unscathed by whatever took the jeep out. It was just another deployment. Bunkers were improved, tents got wooden frames, and the old shower tent graduated to a shower trailer, making it, among other things, harder for Cesar to steal your towel and clothes while you were showering.

We settled in and received our missions from bleary-eyed Operations Officers held upright with coffee and tobacco. Winter Strike 2003 was a go. The entire 75th Ranger Regiment in one place, at one time, on one mission. The last time we were all together was Ranger Rendezvous 2001, a celebration and change of command occurring every two years at Ft. Benning. Rendezvous is replete with sporting competitions, camaraderie, and tomfoolery. Rendezvous 2001 was marked by retiring the black beret that the Army had commandeered and exchanging it for the tan beret. We never could have known our coveted tan berets would become a symbol of transformation over 20 years of war in the desert. Winter Strike 2003 was a significant operation in the early years of that era and was the largest SOF† counterinsurgency operation of the time.

---

* The 75th Ranger Regiment R.I.P. was improved and redesignated to Ranger Assessment and Selection Program (RASP) in the early 2000s and will be referred to as such from here on out.

† Special Operations Forces.

Moving one Ranger Battalion through the mountainous northern region of Afghanistan was a feat unto itself; the Joint Special Operations Task Force moved all three! The initial push was deep into the Hindu Kush mountain range of the Nuristan province through a complex series of C-130 flights, MH-47 lifts, and vehicle convoys. Thousands of Special Operators moved through Jalalabad, Asadabad, and Nangalam, an otherwise forgettable stop on the Pech Valley Road. The Pech Road skirted the Pech River, leaving scant space for towns and villages beneath towering mountains. To the locals, it was home. To us, it was Route Blue, "IED Alley."

Improvised explosive devices (IEDs) became a common issue in the mountainous region. Though the war had just turned two, IED Alley had already claimed countless vehicles and lives from roadside bombs, particularly between checkpoints 2 and 3: Watapur and Nangalam. Just east of Route Blue was our home away from home for the previous spring, Asadabad, a fishbowl, rocket-magnet-of-a-shithole firebase. A-bad got rocketed or mortared four to five times a week by the insurgents running arms and ammunition across the border with Pakistan. At first, you couldn't tell if the explosions were incoming (theirs) or outgoing (ours), but after a few weeks, you learned to tell the difference. You also learned when the incoming fire was close, and when to stay in your rack or get to the bunkers.

We knew the roads of the Kunar and Pech Valleys—the mountains and the villages—inside and out, having spent the bulk of the year negotiating Route Blue at night to avoid mine strikes and providing Quick Reaction Force to units with killed vehicles whose crews insisted on driving during the day. The first rule of traversing Route Blue was identical to the first rule of dealing with explosives: respect it. We had made the long trek back to the Kunar and Pech Valleys, arriving at FOB Catamount in Nangalam, an abandoned Russian outpost from the '80s, now occupied by the 10th Mountain Division. Rangers pooled like brooding waters in a flash flood, ready to break whatever lay in our path. The 75th Ranger Regiment was fully massed for combat for the first time since Operation Just Cause, Panama, in 1989. And my mates and I were right in the middle of it.

Mac and I sat on ammo crates, watching the storm clouds gathering.

"It's like Ranger Rendezvous without sports," I said.

Mac chuckled. He always had a great laugh. I loved getting him going.

"Or beer!" I added.

"Yeah. Shitty Ranger Rendezvous," Mac said.

The lanky North Carolinian and I were squad leaders together for two years before he moved to the Battalion Recce section. Losing Mac was tough. We lost more than just Mac before this deployment, though. Jason had been our Platoon Leader (PL) for two years. The chipper Pennsylvanian was a shade or two from albino with curly blond hair and a cheerful affect. Jason was one of the finest combat leaders I have ever served with. We spent countless patrols together when I was an assault squad leader and he was the command and control. He was dealt a poor hand after OEF 1* when we lost our Platoon Sergeant (PSG), Chad, by accidental discharge during a training exercise. The importance of the PSG cannot be understated. Though he technically reports to the PL, the PSG is the most senior man

---

* Operation Enduring Freedom.

in the platoon by time, experience, capabilities, and competencies. The PSG holds the wisdom and holds the platoon together. There's a reason we call them "Platoon Daddy." Chad was as good as they come—a legend. His replacement was not. Jason, Mac, Tony, me, and Donnie held the platoon together through OEF 2.

Donnie was my cribbage partner and so much more. He taught me a lot. Donnie's squad and I were always teamed up for section patrols once I became the Weapons Squad Leader. As such, I provided the command-and-control element with the machine gun team; Kris, the forward observer; and Charlie, the enlisted tactical air controller (a US Air Force Special Operator). Donnie was the maneuver squad leader with his two fire teams. We were unstoppable in the mountains. One night, we got two hours into a patrol, and a nasty storm popped us in the mouth. We could either head back down the treacherous gains we had fought for or hunker down while the storm passed. We stayed in a hide site all day with sheets of rain screaming sideways across the ground. Donnie kept crawling under my poncho every few hours and saying, "I think it's the tail end of it," with a wry grin. It became a joke for the whole section. We'd troop the line, sidle up next to the boys, and say, "I think it's the tail end of it."

The inside joke persisted through the spring and summer as we kept getting held in place. The command would give us a new redeployment date, then push it back 30 days. "I think it's the tail end of it" became our tagline. Not one storm goes by that I don't think about Donnie and the boys on Nakas Sar. Donnie had also left the platoon by the time of Winter Strike. He got promoted to PSG of 3rd PLT Bravo Company and was leading Rangers one valley away. He would become the Command Sergeant Major of the 2nd Ranger Battalion many years later.

It felt good to be there with Mac on the ammo crates. We didn't have to say much to each other. We had already said so much over the years. We told the boys to rack out while they could while we watched the show. HMMWVs and Toyota Hiluxes were scattered about like a used car lot. Rangers from the 1st Battalion checked vehicles, lashed down supplies, and added sandbags to the floors for blast protection. They had their share of the mission: vehicle convoys as far as they could take us up the Pech Valley to the intersection of the Kantiwa and Parun Valleys. We had ours: search and attack the valleys by foot.

Sitting silently with Mac, the world felt heavy. I had a new PL, a bad Platoon Sergeant, and two new squad leaders on this mission. Thankfully, Tony was still with us. I never felt fully comfortable around the quiet man from SoCal, but I always felt covered. Tony was good. Damned good. And trustworthy. An upside to a shit situation. But me? I wasn't even supposed to be here. I was supposed to be halfway to California by now, on the way to a belated honeymoon to Hawaii and a stateside assignment in Georgia. I took a deep breath and let it out heavily.

"I think it's the tail end of it," Mac said, bumping my knee with his fist. I shook my head and laughed.

The drive up the Pech was uneventful. The boys from 1/75 were pros. They forded rivers and skirted narrow trails while we sat in truck beds and extended cabs. "Get some sleep while you can," the burly 1/75 squad leader said over his shoulder. We had met just hours before when I was assigned to his chalk. Jesse was smart, fierce, and direct. Immediately trustworthy. I knew the type. A Ranger Squad Leader may be the most dangerous man on the battlefield. He is old enough to be wise yet young enough to be reckless at the right time. Guys like Jesse and me spent most of our Squad Leader time in combat, entrusted with essential missions in foreign lands far away from the flagpole. We slept soundly in the care of our brothers from 1/75. Comforted by the bonds of the Ranger Creed, knowing they "will never leave a fallen comrade to fall into the hands of the enemy," and stirred only momentarily when a river fjord slowed the convoy. I heard the gruff squad leader calmly say "Back the fuck up" while pointing a pistol at a local's face. In the lexicon of interlingual relations, everyone speaks gun in your face.

A short time later, an impassable river marked the convoy's end and the foot patrol's beginning. Our brothers kicked out the security perimeter, afforded us time to settle under our rucks, and wished us "good hunting." We climbed into the mountains, progressing to our objective rally point in preparation for our first objective: OBJ Bat. OBJ Bat was a schoolhouse complex long abandoned for the winter. After clearing the complex uneventfully in the night, we occupied by force and established our base of operations in the valley. Though the children had vacated the space, the fleas had not.

We entered the valley just before the snow, but the temperature had already dropped below freezing. Leaving anyone out at night was dangerous. The boys would rotate guard, and we'd troop the line with plumes of hot breath floating on the frigid air. Just another bitter night for the white threaders like me—Winter Ranger School graduates who marked their misery proudly by sewing our Ranger tabs on with white thread. OBJ Bat was another uneventful target chasing ghosts, highlighted by cold, starvation, and flaring tempers. No one from C Co. 2/75 thought we'd be back in Afghanistan so early. Everyone wanted to bring the pain to the enemy. But no enemies were to be found, save for the one straggler with small explosives and a cell phone we snatched up. The Hajis were notorious for using cell phones as detonation devices for roadside bombs. Cold and starvation are notorious for baiting good men into bad behavior.

"Sergeant, you need to see this." One of the boys woke me up from my flea ridden sleep. "Green is beating the prisoner. I think he broke bones."

Green was a Ranger from another platoon. Another good man pushed past his good senses in this bad war. He was tired of being jerked around. Tired of being cold. Tired of being hungry. Tired of being in Afghanistan. I entered the dark room to the smell of urine and sweat. Haji tended to piss himself when he got balled up by Rangers. Especially when he took a black Chinook ride, never to return. The detainee was flex-cuffed and sandbagged with his nose in the corner. Green was wild-eyed and panting.

"Green! Don't lay another hand on the prisoner," I said.

"Fuck this guy!"

"Tell you what, you break one more part of this prisoner, and I'll break your fucking jaw. And it's 'Sergeant' to you, fuckhead!" My eyes were wild now too.

Military bearing has an effective way of jerking soldiers back into reality, especially great soldiers like Green. Anyone in this unit was head and shoulders above their contemporaries. The very best. Great soldiers who committed daily to the part of the Ranger Creed that states, "My courtesy to superior officers, neatness of dress, and care of equipment shall set the example for others to follow."

"Roger, Sergeant!" Green said. He was back, and the discussion was over. And I was going back to my flea-ridden fart-sack.*

---

* Sleeping bag.

The following week was a blur. We patrolled north through the valley, clearing small clusters of buildings that clung to mountainsides like a baby on her mother's chest. The snow floated a blanket of white over our tan DCUs* and mud rooftops. Deeper into the cold and the mountains, the cloud ceiling eliminated any hope of close air support. The clouds were only half the problem. Aircraft lift capability decreases when the temperature drops and the altitude increases. For the first time in three rotations, we were truly on our own. Another first in my Army career: we built fires in the field inside of low barns to fend off frostbite. I couldn't help but laugh at the irony. Countless training missions under pouring Pacific Northwest rain, airfield seizures on the frozen desert floor of Idaho, and long winter nights in Yakima had taught us to suck up the cold.

In Afghanistan—in combat—the cold would have injured Rangers, and we had scant options for extraction. We had to adjust smartly or face the consequences of unforced errors. We commandeered barns after clearing villages and made them our safe havens from the cold, nestled in with the goats, the chickens . . . and the fleas. Poor Will's stomach looked like a colorblindness test, his pale white skin dotted with dark red bites. He never once complained. The skinny West Virginian just kept humping the largest gun in the platoon and waited for his chance to unleash hell on our enemies.

A small apartment in the middle of Kantiwa became the platoon CP† for a few days as we cleared towns and villages from the valley floor to the ridgeline. The farther north we climbed, the farther from

---

* Desert Camouflage Uniforms.

† Command post.

our support system we traveled. With the altitude and the cold, our trusted helicopters could bring us neither close air support nor aerial resupply. The prospect of getting Rangers the calories needed to sustain the effort became a daily mission of its own. One section per day patrolled south to where the Kantiwa and Parun Valleys intersected, where the Battalion CP was positioned along with a makeshift HLZ* for resupply. We gathered men, weapons, equipment, and a train of donkeys for the patrol. A blanket of snow covered the ground, with average temperatures in the 20s. Though the conditions were miserable, they afforded us a degree of security. We learned early in the war about Haji what our forefathers had learned about Charlie in Vietnam. Haji does not need to make peace with misery in his land. He has the benefit of time on his side. We had the mastery of suffering.

Rangers enter denied areas, bed down in swamps, and turn snow-covered mountain valleys into throughways at 7,500 feet. It's part of our heritage going back to the Revolutionary War's Francis Marion, "The Swamp Fox," whose life inspired the movie *The Patriot*. Every day, a squad of Rangers covered the growing distance down the valley to our support as the Company cleared farther north. Ten kilometers, twelve kilometers, fifteen kilometers. The distance increased, but the rations remained the same: one meal per man per day. When not tasked with the resupply patrol, we climbed ice chutes up to towns and villages at 11,000 feet, hopeful to see blue sky through cloud fall but routinely disappointed at the top. Upon entering the villages, we executed a classic Ranger raid with support and maneuver elements doing what Rangers do best (aside from suffering, that is).

---

* Helicopter landing zone.

Snow hugged my knees while the altitude squeezed my chest as I heaved through every three- to five-second rush across those villages. I had won the Glenn E. Morrell Army Physical Fitness Award at the Basic Noncommissioned Officer Course a year prior, running a personal record 10:05 2-mile. I was fit and fast. But the mountain breaks everyone. These mountains have seen hundreds of expeditionary forces like us. They were not impressed by my speed on asphalt at sea level. The locals, on the other hand, were not as glib. They crumpled into corners with shrieks and wails as we kicked in doors. Their eyes betrayed the shock of our presence in their remote village; our gray faces hid equal amazement that someone actually lived up here. Wet boots and dry holes were all we found, along with another feather in our suffering hats.

One useless raid after another made us question our intel and our leaders who sent us here. The cold was not the only bitterness descending upon our platoon. Rangers are notorious for being tough *and* smart. After spending nearly two years busting down dry holes, the boys and I began to wonder what kind of war this was. Regardless of the kind of war or the level of satisfaction gained by it, war always reminds us of its grotesqueness. For two years, we had been lucky. The 2nd Ranger Battalion had deployed consistently since the beginning of 2002, conducting missions in Afghanistan and Iraq without a KIA.* The Pech Valley put an end to that. Crammed into our makeshift CP for the night with a pot-belly furnace and MRE† hot cocoa, tonight's Battalion update on command satellite radio was different. The Battalion Commander's monotone voice shared one KIA,

---

* Killed in action.

† Meal Ready to Eat (ration).

multiple wounded, and a destroyed vehicle. Jay Anthony Blessing was killed by a roadside bomb on November 14, 2003.

Jay was a beautiful artist with a wry smile and a sarcastic wit. When he went to Ranger School, he struggled in Mountain Phase but refused to give up. When he finally buckled, they discovered he had been suffering from pneumonia and a collapsed lung. When they sent Jay home to Ft. Lewis, WA, he recovered slowly under the mentorship of Battalion legend and retired Marine Mr. Ray Fuller in the Battalion Arms Room. Jay soaked up every drop of knowledge he could gather from the old Marine and kept the Battalion's heavy guns operational. Jay would not accept defeat and returned to Ranger School, grinding through the suck to reach the "Ranger objective." His body once again rejected the circumstances, but his resolve rejected failure. Jay limped into graduation with yet another case of pneumonia and lung complications and earned his Ranger tab. Mission complete. He was on his way to the Special Forces Qualification Course when we got alerted for the Winter Strike 2003. He could have stayed back. Jay deployed.

Stunned by the news, I sat in silence.

Holy shit, I thought. *Holy shit.*

War sucks. We would never see Jay again. Nor would his parents. And the loss left an indelible mark on the Rangers, who were there picking up the pieces. I could only imagine. I didn't want to imagine. I had to imagine. I had to try to make sense of how we could lose one of our Rangers over the seemingly irrelevant mission value thus far. These valleys, these villages, the fleas, the starvation, the hundred-pound rucks with the requirement to carry one WWII-era tripod even though the mountains made them useless. Insanity! All the while, my wife was home alone for as long as the Army deemed and potentially forever. Left to raise our baby, tend to our home, and make do with the Army's schedule and her husband's "mission critical" status on a useless mission. It was all too much. I wanted to go home. In a box or on my feet. I didn't care. I just wanted it to stop.

"Where you headed, Sergeant?" Matt said.

I realized that I was putting my gear on only after he spoke. Matt was sitting on the dusty floor of the little apartment. He was a reliable Ranger who kept our jeep on four wheels and us on course more times than I could count. And I couldn't count more times than I care to admit because I couldn't stay awake on many of those long drives.

"I'm going to go check the guns," I said.

Matt looked up at me with his keen eyes. He looked *into* me. He looked across the hooch at our Platoon Sergeant, then back at me. The PSG was scrunched into a small corner eating chow from his second MRE of the day, though the boys were sharing a packet of hot cocoa from our one. Our platoon was already hanging on by a thread.

"Troop the line," I said. We held there for a moment.

"Roger, Sergeant," Matt replied.

That night, I walked from position to position in Kantiwa South, checking on security but mostly checking on the boys. From low cattle barns with fires that forced you to duck-walk under the smoke to little hide sites in the snow, Rangers were doing what Rangers do—protecting one another and manning their posts. I loved them. I love them. They gave me strength and they gave me purpose. They gave me a reason to go one more day even though I felt the weight of the world upon my shoulders in this shithole country. The weight of our small world of Rangers, the Madslashers, also held me up when

23

I needed it most. You know you're in the throes of adversity when a sense of helplessness and the fear of hopelessness strike. The boys gave me a reason to persevere.

"Readily will I display the intestinal fortitude required to fight on to the Ranger objective and complete the mission, though I be the lone survivor."[*]

PART II: THE SHEGAL VALLEY

We returned from Kantiwa three weeks later and 30 pounds lighter with gaunt faces and threadbare uniforms. We knew we had accomplished something by the looks on everyone's faces when we walked through the compound. We thought we would download ammo and go home. Clearly, Winter Strike was a failure since no one had killed a single enemy, yet we had taken one KIA. But that was not the case. The command to refit for round two came quickly. We tossed our flea-ridden uniforms, set the boys in motion, and made our way to the air mission briefings.

The helicopter insertion was going to be a mess. I had seen this story before: 60-foot treetops would prohibit our aircraft from touching the ramp down on the ridgeline for a smooth infill. We were headed into the Shegal Valley, Kunar Province. As the aircraft leader for 20 Special Operators, I did my final checks, ready for a fight and weighted down to sustain another month in the mountains. Tucked between the mountaintops, the Shegal Valley cut a line in the sand between the Taliban and the coalition objectives intended to stabilize

---

[*] Sixth stanza of the Ranger Creed.

Afghanistan. Within that valley, a high-ranking Taliban leader was coordinating strikes across the Pakistan border (an imaginary line on the map that meant nothing to the locals). We got the call and got to work. We would insert into blocking positions on the ridgeline and gain overwatch to enable a SEAL platoon to move from compound to compound in search of our target.

―――――

Perched on a knee at the back of the ramp with my chalk co-leader, Jon, I watch the ridgeline come closer through my NODs.* The blackness is stolen through the pixelated green screen highlighted by dots of stars across the night sky. As the bird ambles toward the world, I am calm. I have to be. The boys behind me depend upon it. The ground comes closer and into focus while the air mission brief just eight hours before replays in my mind.

"We're going to try our best to touch the ramp down so you guys can run off," the pilot had said as we crowded over an aerial imagery map in the tactical operations center.

"Briefs well!" I'd replied with a smirk. Everyone can see that big chip on my shoulder. It's my edge and my downfall. And I'm in no mood to soften it based on the previous month. I shouldn't even be here.

"The treetops are too high for that. You'll never be able to get the ramp that close with the rotors turning," I'd continued. Jon had looked over the map with me quietly. A new squad leader to our platoon on this deployment, he has already proven his mettle in spades. He is smart, strong, and steady—a true rock for the guys and me. Jon

―――――――――――――――

* Night Optical Device.

25

and I had bonded quickly over scant plates of beans and our care for the boys the previous month in the mountains. I wasn't so alone with guys like Jon on the leadership team.

"We're going to do our best," the pilot had repeated. He was sincere, and we all knew why. The worst-case scenario is trying to fast-rope onto the top of the jagged rock face.

"We'll make sure the ropes are ready in case we need them," the crew chief said.

"Roger," I replied. No one was interested in arguing, and I was too tired to bother. "We know you're the best in the world," I said. "If anyone can touch a bird down on the Shegal, it's you. We'll be ready to rope if we need to."

Back on the ramp, the rocks outside are so close that I can see the underbrush gripping the ridgeline from the force of the rotor wash. My breathing slows, and I make my final preparations, reciting Psalm 23 and a prayer. The heat of the rotor wash bounces off the rocks into the ramp with the smell of burning jet fuel. I count the rocks and recheck my weapon as the bird stabilizes. Almost there. My hand grips the snap link to detach my safety line. Strength and honor. Almost there.

The aircraft suddenly pitches forward, and I am weightless. The floor underneath me disappears. I am suspended in the air. Held inside the bird by my safety line and snap link. My teeth pulverize my jaw. I flail near the open ramp. The bright green stars blur across my narrowing field of vision. Swimming for the side of the fuselage, I grasp it with my hand. Through the open ramp, the world spins between the mountain and the sky. We are hurtling toward the Shegal Valley in a spinning MH-47. Game over. Breathing in the centrifugal force and out my last thoughts, I consider Jaden, and I think of Kelly. I'm never going to see my son again. "God, please save us!" I pray. This isn't the first time I've been close to death, but I am confident it will be my last.

As I pray, caught between the ground and the sky, the force crushes my chest and skull. The engines scream—their power fighting to rip the aircraft from the pull of the mountains. My vision narrows to a point. Almost there.

The engines roar to a crescendo. They feel like they are between my ears. But the spinning sky slows as my vision begins to widen again. I feel my feet on the metal surface of the fuselage. I feel my breath return. I feel the air beneath the helicopter. And I know we've got to get the hell out of this bird!

We move fast. Within a minute, the bird hovers above the treetops, the fast ropes are kicked out, and Jon and I peer into the blackness over the ramp to confirm the ropes are on the ground. With one hand on the rope, Jon and I look back at each other for a thumbs-up.

We lock gazes an arm's length apart. Two young leaders with 20 lives counting on us and a mission waiting for us. The enemy doesn't care how scary the insertion has been thus far, nor can we. In unison, we shrug our shoulders as if to say, "Fuck it," give the thumbs-up, and rotate out into the night. "Follow me!"

We are heavy, and the rope is long. Too long. We rocket toward the mountain loaded with a month's worth of supplies. Before I hit the ground, I am struck in the face. Hard. The machine gun barrel of the man behind me crushes my NODs mount and the bridge of my nose. I hold tight to the rope, my lifeline to the earth, and continue to slide, dazed and angry. I hit the dirt and slide. Down the mountain I go. The man behind me, Paul, breaks his ankle upon impact. Another Ranger misses the rope and burns in, breaking his back.

The insertion is a disaster. We are scattered across the mountainside with a mission to conduct and a casualty that needs immediate extraction. We gather ourselves into two elements and move one into our blocking position and another into a security posture to call a MEDEVAC.* Paul moves with me to the blocking position—the pain must have been unbearable. All he says is, "I'm sorry about your nose, Sergeant."

———

When the sun rose, we had an extracted casualty, a banged-up platoon, and a bird's-eye view over the valley. Strong-pointed on all sides, the SEALs flew from compound to compound in search of our target. When their mission was completed, they flew away, leaving us to continue ours. The following weeks were highlighted by more of the same. We got a break in the midst of the operation when the Command flew out Thanksgiving chow. We huddled around little fires and shared what we were thankful for over turkey and mashed potatoes. A subtle middle finger to these mountains and their people. You can throw what you like at us; we will not break.

I sat between my friend Josh (our mortars section leader for all these rotations) and my Ranger Buddy, Justin—we had been side by side since the day I became a Ranger. I always felt a little lighter with Justin. Thankful for his smile and his smarts. Thankful for his friendship. Thankful that six years prior I was assigned to him as his Ranger Buddy. Since that day we had sweat together, fought together, cried together, and led together. To this day, we do life together still.

———

* Medical evacuation; extraction of a casualty.

The following week, a lone rocketeer fired a one-in-a-million shot across the valley and nearly killed Jon W., the indomitable team leader with the devious smile. A young Ranger had joined the platoon just weeks before we deployed and froze on the machine gun, failing to return fire. Justin and I took the M240B and returned fire on cyclic, kicking off a barrage of machine gun fire that was done (for the most part) in frustration. All we had was a perceived location from the rocket's contrail. All we needed was an excuse to release our anger.

That night, we kicked in doors and shook the foundations of the village across the river. Terror is the only thing I recall from the faces of the villagers. I wanted to kill every one of them. But I never once pulled the trigger inside the village. None of us did. Though we pained about the loss of Jay and burned with fury for our country, our families, and our situation, we remained "morally straight." Our Ranger creed demanded it be so. And our circumstances continually gave us opportunities to become the creed, one mission at a time.

In the morning, 1SG G. called me to the company CP and sat me down. My Platoon Sergeant sat in the background of the dusty hut, looking at his feet. 1SG G. looked at me and said, "Staff Sergeant Young, you're taking the platoon on this next push up the valley. We're clearing the next three gridlines. I'll roll with you."

"What about him?" I asked.

"SSG Young, you're taking the platoon on this next push up the valley," 1SG G. replied.

"Roger, First Sergeant," I said.

Many gridlines, villages, and a month later, we returned to Ft. Lewis. No fanfare. No applause. No parade. We downloaded our gear, put on civvies, and went home. 1SG G. pulled me aside and said, "You did a great job out there, Ranger." We shook hands and said good-bye.

Over the next few weeks, I didn't see the guys at all. Kel and I packed up the house. I turned in my gear and left the 2nd Ranger Battalion, my home. My family. The last time I saw the Madslashers together in one place was in the platoon hallway of the old C Co. barracks. The boys knew I was on a sprint to catch up to my orders and make a belated honeymoon trip to Hawaii. Jon asked me to stop by before leaving Washington. The platoon gathered in the hallway and said thank you as warriors do—with a custom 1911 pistol and the incalculable respect and love that it relayed. My mission was complete.

Sometimes, the last thing that you want to do is the next thing you need to do. I didn't want to deploy to Winter Strike. I didn't want to troop the line after Jay was killed. I didn't want to load up for the Shegal after returning from Kantiwa. I didn't want to fast-rope after holding on inside a spinning Chinook. But I did. Every setback was a decision: respond or react; quit or persevere. We persevered. And we did it together, accomplishing our mission along with it. Perseverance calls us to become the leaders the situation demands to accomplish the missions that are needed the most. We don't get to choose the time when destiny calls us into who we were created to be. We just get to choose whether or not to answer when it does.

2

Nobody Goes Undefeated in Life

BLAYNE SMITH

I f you are reasonably talented and lucky enough to grow up in a safe, supportive environment, you can get pretty deep into life without major setbacks. Bombing a math test or getting cut from the varsity team may feel like serious failures to a driven high-school kid, but those moments are merely practice for life's real adversity.

In January 2009, my Special Forces team and I landed at Firebase Anaconda in an extremely remote district of Afghanistan's Uruzgan Province. I hit the ground as a 30-year-old West Point graduate who had consistently taken on the most difficult courses and assignments and excelled in every one of them. I expected this deployment to be no different. I was wrong.

By February 20, five of my teammates were dead, another seriously wounded, and the rest of us were absolutely reeling. As the firebase commander, I was completely responsible for this calamity and for finding a path forward. Somehow, I had to muster the calm and clarity to make sound decisions and motivate my team to stay in the fight, which was awfully difficult given that a big part of me just wanted to curl up in a ball and quit. I was devastated and scared. For the first time in my life, I truly felt like a failure.

Nothing had or could have prepared me for this situation—not West Point or Ranger School or Special Forces training or even my previous combat tour in Iraq. This was beyond my experience . . . beyond the experience of anybody that I knew. I felt like, despite my successful background and a whole battalion of Green Berets around me, I had nothing to really lean on.

I woke up on the morning of February 12 brimming with confidence and ready to take on the world. Eight days later, the world (and the Taliban) had shown me that I wasn't. I had learned the very hard lesson that nobody goes undefeated in life. And whoever I'd been when I landed at Firebase Anaconda was not going to be the guy who saw us through this tragedy. That guy was not capable of handling such immense loss and uncertainty. I would have to change, grow, and become the person my team needed me to be.

———

It is very difficult for words to capture the bond that Special Forces teammates share. We may describe ourselves as brothers, but it's something different, something more.

When I showed up to the 3rd Special Forces Group in late March 2007, I was fresh out of Ranger School, 15 pounds underweight, and eager to make a dent in the universe. After more than two years of training, it was finally time to lead a team of Green Berets. But things went a little slower than I was hoping for. The battalion had just returned from a deployment to Afghanistan, and there would now be several months of what the Army calls "re-fit." More than half of my A-Team, or ODA, was turning over, and it would take some time for it to come together and for me to find the new crew's personality. And it would take even longer for us to build the kind of reputation that would earn us the assignments we all wanted. During one of my first talks with the team, I told them there would be no magic bullets and no elevator to the top of the mountain. There was no chance the president would ring us up and tell us to capture Osama bin Laden. No, our path to greatness would be a long, deliberate march. We were going to demonstrate our commitment to excellence in all of the small ways—by being brilliant in the basics. We started that day by (and I'm not kidding) cleaning the team room.

Our ODA did hundreds of "little" things right during the next few months. The Special Forces is a very autonomous environment. Teams are trusted to train and prepare with limited supervision from higher headquarters. Some ODAs will take advantage of the opportunity to do a bit less. We took it as an opportunity to do more. We showed up for physical training every morning at 6 AM and got after it—running, rucking, CrossFit, swimming, combatives, all of it. We executed every shooting range with professionalism and urgency. If one of our guys went to a training course like Sniper School, we expected him to finish at the top of the class. We held ourselves to high standards and competed relentlessly. And it didn't take very long for people to start noticing. By the end of 2007, our team had moved much closer to the top of the heap, and we were finally assigned our first "cool" mission.

---

* Operational Detachment—Alpha.

We loaded our gear in the spring of 2008 to set out for Fort A. P. Hill, Virginia. A three-letter agency had requested support in developing and executing an assessment and training program for a select group of agents that would be conducting operations in hostile areas abroad. Our team was asked if we could create a six-week program, acquire the necessary resources, coordinate all the logistics, and execute the training all by ourselves. I can't remember our exact response, but I recall it being something like "too easy."

Over the course of that mission and many other training evolutions, our ODA was forged into one of the battalion's strongest and most capable teams. We spent long days and weeks preparing ourselves for what was ahead, often living and working in miserable conditions. Most of it was done quietly, focusing on the not-so-sexy aspects of the Special Forces mission, like practicing down-driver drills in HMMWVs or loading frequencies into radios. Nobody needed to motivate us; we knew that our training would be tested. We knew that we were headed for Firebase Anaconda.

Firebase Anaconda was located in a remote river valley of the Uruzgan Province of southern Afghanistan. And by remote, I mean 90 kilometers from the nearest friendly position and no road to get there. It was a small outpost, only about 200 × 200 meters, with mountains rising on all sides. Leading up to the deployment, we were in constant contact with the ODA that we were relieving. They shared their daily intelligence and situation reports, which painted a frightening picture of the situation on the ground. During the summer and fall of 2008, the Taliban offensive in the area had been aggressive and constant. The team had been attacked nearly every time they left the walls of the firebase, resulting in dozens of intense firefights and

9 out of the 12 members of the ODA earning Purple Hearts. It became clear that this deployment was not a drill and not a joke. We were in for a tough fight against a determined enemy and would have to bring our very best. Yet despite the horrifying reports from Anaconda, we were eager, even excited to get there. This is what we'd all signed up for. Confidence was high.

———

Our two CH-47 Chinooks dropped into the valley, and we got our first look at our home for the next six months. It was a bluebird day in late January. The air was freezing cold and amazingly fresh as it blew through the helicopter. Suddenly, our long casual flight from Kandahar Airfield (KAF) shifted gears. We flew low and fast across the high-desert floor. We came up on the east side of the firebase and banked sharply to the left. The village of Khas Uruzgan came into view, a large blue minaret marking the mosque at the center. Seeing it with my own eyes for the first time was bizarre, almost like landing on a movie set. I couldn't believe how tiny the base was and how close it was to the village. You could literally throw a rock from one to the other.

In an instant, the helicopters pitched hard, noses to the sky, ramps toward the ground. We landed and started filing off the aircraft, grabbing gear and chucking it onto the makeshift gravel helipad. A couple of guys from the team we were replacing helped us unload. They were very happy to do so, as this was their ride home, what we called "The Freedom Bird." Once everything was off, our counterparts gave me a quick handshake, boarded the helicopter, and said, "Good luck!" That was it.

The birds took off and faded into the distance. Things went quiet, and there we were. All of my senses were alive and stimulated. The cold air was still on my face, but the freshness was gone as the smell of dogs, goats, and burning trash filled my nose. The view of the valley from the ground was intimidating. It felt like being at the bottom of a barrel. Hills and mountains rose steeply to the north, east, and west, while the village sat just beyond the southern wall. Watchtowers marked all four corners of the base, and you could tell that they weren't just there for show. It all gave me the overwhelming feeling of being surrounded.

We linked up with a handful of Americans who were held over from the previous crew, including Tim, an Air Force combat controller who'd spent more than 12 months at Anaconda. We also got to know our counterparts from the Czech Special Forces, who were 45 members strong and came with excellent training and experience. Last, we spent some time meeting our host-nation Afghan partners. Living on the base with us were 50 Afghan Security Guards (ASG), mostly local Hazara villagers who had been harshly oppressed under the Taliban regime. They were solid tacticians and loyal comrades, and while you can't ever share complete trust in that kind of environment, the ASG had proven very dependable. There were also about a hundred soldiers from the Afghan National Army (ANA) who lived in a small compound up the hill. The ANA was much less professional and reliable. It consisted of young, poorly trained men from around the country, and unlike the ASG, whose families lived in the area, they had little commitment to the mission. Still, it was our job to train and fight alongside them because that is what Green Berets do. We had our work cut out for us.

The firebase had a steady rotation of visitors, too, including the local Afghan National Police chief, the district governor, and other local "personalities." After only about a week on the ground, my days were filled with nearly constant requests for somebody to meet with "Captain Blayne." I drank what seemed like a hundred cups of chai a day and lived with a continuous caffeine buzz.

At the southwest corner of the base, we ran a clinic, or MED-CAP,* a few days a week, providing the only real medical care in the area. Our medics, Marc and Linsey, would see upwards of 50 patients a day with ailments and injuries of all sorts, including some stuff that we don't typically see in the developed world. The stories from the clinic were epic: some hilarious, others absolutely tragic.

When stationed at a remote firebase, ODAs have a lot to do. My team sergeant, Dave, and I had a plan coming in. The idea was to spend the first few months building capacity and creating some "white space," or reasonably safe terrain around the firebase and village. We knew that while the Taliban were still active during the cold winter months, they would likely become much more aggressive when the weather warmed up in the spring and summer, during what was often referred to as "the Fighting Season" in southern Afghanistan. Our goal was to execute simultaneously across several "lines of effort," meaning that every single mission had to serve multiple operational objectives. For example, a standard combat reconnaissance patrol might serve to check out a potential future target (combat operations) while also stopping to inspect a micro-hydroelectric plant that we helped pay for (civil–military operations). On the way back, we might also visit a nearby village to drop off some humanitarian assistance while secretly meeting with an informant (intelligence operations). Of course, we'd do this alongside our Afghan Army counterparts to help

---

* Medical Capabilities.

them develop their tactical skills during a relatively simple mission (training operations), and we might even make a short radio broadcast about the "Afghan-led security operation" upon returning to base (information operations).

Our approach yielded some success during our first few weeks on the ground. We were getting a feel for our Afghan partners, building our intelligence network, and establishing rapport with the local community. It felt like we had a pretty solid handle on things. Still, we knew that we were far from safe. The Taliban were always watching and would chatter on their radios whenever we were out and about, and though we had yet to be directly engaged, we suspected it was only a matter of time.

––––––

It was rainy and cold on the morning of February 12. We had to delay the start of our mission due to thick fog in the early hours. We almost decided not to go at all that day. Finally, at about 10 AM, we launched out of the north gate of Anaconda and headed east toward a narrow mountain pass that led to the small village of Faramuz. We planned to patrol into the village, establish a security perimeter, and try to talk to a few of the locals. We'd received some information that a Taliban bomb maker had set up shop in one of the mud huts, and there might even be some explosives cached in the area.

As we deliberately made our way into the pass, we started hearing Taliban radio chatter. They were tracking our movements closely and seemed to be watching us from at least two vantage points in the hills above. It was normal for the locals and Taliban to report on our movements, and while it wasn't shocking to hear the radio chatter, it never felt good. Our gunners scanned the terrain with their optics to try and identify the observers. Though we knew we were under surveillance, we proceeded, pulling into Faramuz and positioning our trucks in a defensive posture around the village. I hopped out and, along with a few other guys, went over to talk with a few villagers who came out to meet us.

We had just concluded a meeting when the Taliban chatter really picked up.

"Do you want me to start?"

"Do you want me to do work on the Americans?"

Seconds later, a bullet snapped between me and my intel sergeant, Gus. Another cracked over our heads. The ground began exploding upwards in muddy raindrops as bullets flew from the ridge above. We ran back to our truck to direct fire and radio for air support. Our driver, Bob, returned fire from behind his armored door while our tail gunner, Josh, angled his M240 for a better shot. Everybody was shouting, but I couldn't make out any of it. Casey, our turret gunner, was pounding the ridgeline, and the sound of the .50-caliber machine gun was deafening. I grabbed his leg—"You gotta stop for a minute!"—and then yelled over to Bob, "What are you trying to tell me!?" His response was finally clear.

"Marc got shot in the face!"

I couldn't tell what was really going on, so I took off running back up the hill toward Marc's truck. It couldn't have been more than 150 yards, but it felt like it took me forever to get there. My feet kept slipping on the wet ground, and my lungs burned from the eight thousand feet of elevation. When I finally got there, I saw Marc lying on his back, perfectly still. Linsey was frantically working on him, but I could tell that it was futile. I had expected to see Marc hunched over, holding a bleeding wound, expected to tell him to get his ass in the truck. But Marc wasn't blinking, and there wasn't much blood. His beard and scarf hid the entry point of the bullet near his chin.

Oh my God. He's dead.

Later that night, I cried in front of the team. I couldn't help it. I loved Marc; we all did. He was the quintessential Green Beret—smart, funny, sarcastic, and exceptionally skilled at every single aspect of being a medic and a soldier. He was the very best of us, and in an instant, he was gone. His death profoundly impacted everybody. It was a miserable feeling, and it was hard to imagine anything worse. But it would get worse, much worse.

Eight days later, on the day of Marc's funeral, we launched a seemingly simple operation to secure a fjord site for our Czech counterparts. They were doing a long patrol and needed some support in crossing a swift river near the village of Char Asyab. It was a precarious section of their route, and we wanted them to be able to keep moving without getting bogged down and being susceptible to an ambush.

Our convoy of five vehicles moved toward the river from the north, traveling slowly down a narrow dirt path. To our left, the ground sloped sharply to the river below. To our right, the mountains shot steeply toward the sky. We were just approaching the fjord site and preparing to stop when I heard—and felt—an enormous boom behind me. At almost exactly the same time, a rocket-propelled grenade came screaming toward my truck and exploded into the rock wall in front of us. A panicked voice came over the radio: "Truck three is destroyed. Truck three is completely destroyed!"

Machine gun fire erupted from the river below. It was a coordinated ambush. There was a raging river to our front, a burning HMMWV blocking the path behind us, and Taliban all around us. We were sitting ducks.

A massive roadside bomb had flipped truck three over and blown its turret gunner nearly 30 feet into the air. Eric spun like a rag doll and landed hard, shattering his right leg and injuring his back. Linsey ran through small-arms fire to drag Eric away from the raging fireball as ammunition and explosives began cooking off in all directions. Then he went right back into it.

Linsey found our team sergeant, Dave, on his hands and knees behind the burning wreck; he'd been blown free of his passenger seat but got caught in the flash. His boots and flame-retardant uniform were mostly intact, but he was badly burned. Linsey bent down and somehow had the presence of mind to ask if he could walk. Unable to talk, Dave nodded. We all knew that Dave was tough as hell, but to walk away from that was beyond belief. Linsey guided him through a hail of bullets to the back of his truck and put an IV in Dave's foot. For a while, we thought that the legend of Dave Hurt would have another unbelievable chapter, but he would succumb to his wounds later that night.

Once Eric and Dave were loaded up, I told Gus to drive them down the river and help set up a MEDEVAC site. Then I told him to please remember to come back for us.

The three of us left on the scene started trying to secure the wreckage of truck three and look for our other teammates. We found Tim first. He was just uphill from the truck, flat on his back. He looked okay at first glance, but he wasn't. The blast had likely killed him instantly, blowing off his kit and taking part of his right leg.

We found our interpreter, Eman, next. He'd also been thrown clear and lay dead with barely a scratch on him, his signature Nike beanie still on his head.

Where was Jeremy? He'd been driving the truck when it was struck but now was nowhere to be seen. Between fighting back the ambush and securing loose weapons and equipment, we kept searching for him. Finally, David, our senior weapons sergeant, figured it out. He waved me over and pointed to the burning hulk. Jeremy was in there. You could barely make him out. David used a pry bar to lift part of the flaming mass while I put on a pair of asbestos mittens and carefully pulled him out.

That was four men dead in a matter of seconds, bringing our total now to five. This was my responsibility. For a few moments, I wished that a Taliban would just take me out too. It would be easier than dealing with whatever would be next.

———

In the days following February 20, the overarching sensation among the team was numbness. It was such an unimaginable scenario that we couldn't even process it. And though you talk about, and to some extent prepare for, the possibility of losing a teammate in combat, the reality of losing five guys in eight days was totally bewildering. We spent a week or so just going through the motions, packing up our friends' gear, accounting for sensitive items, and filling out sworn statements. None of us had much of a sense of where to go from here. This shit definitely wasn't in the brochure. At some point, the speculation started.

"They're definitely going to send us home."

"No way. They'll just send another team out here to reinforce us."

"I think they're gonna pull us to KAF and let us hang out for the rest of the trip."

The questions of what would happen next tactically were somewhat worrisome, but we all had even bigger questions in our minds.

"Am I going to die out here?"

"How will I ever manage to live with this on my conscience?"

"What the hell are we even doing this for?"

It felt like everything that we thought we knew about everything had just been thrown in a blender and poured out all over the floor. The future had no shape to it. That kind of uncertainty is utterly and completely terrifying, especially for a bunch of folks who pride themselves on thriving in austere environments. If there had been a clear way to proceed, even if incredibly difficult, every one of us would have put our heads down and sucked it up. But this wasn't that kind of hard. This was totally different from gutting out a long ruck march during SF Assessment and Selection or surviving days of torture at SERE School. To get through it, we didn't just need to decide what to do; we needed to decide who we were.

I finally realized that the Task Force headquarters would probably take their cues from us. I was the unit commander, and I needed to make a recommendation about what to do next. It was clear that the guys were all dealing with things in their own ways. Some were obviously shaken, some were calm, and some were angry. The one thing we shared was that we all wanted to be together.

The most significant practical decision we needed to make was whether to try and stay at Anaconda or have another ODA come out and replace us so that we could return to Kandahar, regroup, and take on a different mission set. I wasn't sure what to do. I was torn. My ego absolutely wanted to stay at the firebase for another five months and figure out a way to kill every single member of the Taliban that we could find. My heart wanted to fold up shop and do everything I could to keep anybody else from getting hurt. My head said that the best course of action was probably somewhere in between.

One night, I grabbed two of my teammates to talk it over. I needed to get some additional perspective, especially concerning how the guys were holding up. Casey and Gus were two of my most capable and trusted NCOs, and I knew they would assess the situation honestly and thoughtfully. I offered them a couple of potential ways that we could approach the rest of the trip. We could stay at Anaconda, have some additional Green Berets come out to shore us up, and stick it out until July. Or we could request to be relieved, hand the mission off to another ODA, and go back to Kandahar to work on the Afghan Commando training mission, which would allow us some time to recover before returning into full combat operations.

Both of these options felt incredibly difficult. On one hand, the idea of staying out there, stunned and degraded, was harrowing to say the least. On the other hand, the notion that our team could be "blown out of our firebase" was a result that I wasn't sure any of us could stomach. It felt like we had no good options, but we had a choice to make.

It was when Casey, who was always calm and confident, told me, "I gotta be honest, I'm pretty fucked up," that I knew what I had to do. The next morning, I got on the phone with our Task Force commander and gave him my recommendation: to swap us out with another team and pull us back to Kandahar. I did not want to walk down this path, but it was the only way forward.

A couple of weeks later, we hit the ground at our new home and started to settle in. We needed to make a fresh start, which was a huge ask of a group of people who had just experienced such a profound loss. I think we might have been forgiven for simply mailing it in and doing the bare minimum for the remainder of the deployment. Heck, we might have even been encouraged to do so, as I'm sure that the brass didn't want to have to explain to our families why yet another guy from ODA 3123 was coming home wounded or dead. But as I tactfully reminded the team (and myself), we were soldiers, we were at war, and it was our duty to get back in the fight.

This was not how anybody imagined the deployment going. None of us wanted things to be the way they were. And while the horror and pain of what happened at Anaconda was still present in our dreams every night, we woke up each morning to a new and unplanned reality. There was nothing we could do to change the past, no way to replay those events or bring our friends back. But there was a way to conduct ourselves that would honor their memories and their sacrifice. We had to accept the fact that the Taliban were still out there, growing stronger as the weather warmed up, and it was our job to try and stop them. Soon, we would be given a chance.

The other team that was working on the Afghan Commando mission was led by a guy named KC, and in addition to being a tremendous combat leader, he was also a very good friend. He was well aware of what had happened at Anaconda and understood that our team was shaken but needed to get back on the horse. So, in a move that I will always remember and never be able to repay, he told the Task Force that his team needed our ODA to join them on an upcoming mission.

The Taliban had completely taken over a village in the northern Helmand Province and were using it to produce hundreds of bombs and tons of black tar opium. The mission called for about 50 Green Berets and Afghan Commandos, along with a few interagency partners, to fly into the village under the cover of darkness, hit two high-value targets, and be out of there in less than two hours. It felt like an amazing opportunity for our team to get back in the action, build a bit of confidence, and set ourselves up for the rest of the deployment. If everything went according to plan, we'd have high-fives and beers for breakfast.

At exactly 1:03 AM, our MH-53s landed in a big poppy field adjacent to the village's bazaar. The assault teams ran down the ramps and quickly established a security perimeter. Through my night vision goggles, I could see our assigned target, lit up by a giant infrared spotlight shining down from a drone that was circling above. We established radio checks, confirmed our avenue of approach, and began moving briskly toward the breach point. The night was totally black, what we called "zero-illum," and the village seemed very quiet, almost abandoned.

We could all hear ourselves breathing inside of our headphones. It was dead quiet as teams of assaulters took up positions near the doors of the target buildings. The call came over the radio: "At my command, 5, 4, 3, 2, 1, initiate . . ."

Boom! Simultaneously, a series of breaching charges exploded, and we flooded into the buildings. The next few minutes were controlled chaos as operators flowed through the buildings, clearing rooms and ultimately securing the objectives. Then more calls over the radio: *"Jackpot!"*

Both targets had what we came for—one a bomb-making factory and the other a massive store of opium. The bombs were doubtlessly

46

being shipped out across southern Afghanistan, taking countless coalition lives. And the black tar opium was fueling the Taliban's lucrative heroin trade, which financed much of their operation. It was a big win and not a particularly difficult one. We could almost taste the cold beer. Unfortunately, the win was *too* big. Our comeback tour wasn't going to be so easy after all.

The next radio call I heard was from up in Bagram at the Combined Joint Special Operations Task Force. The commander had been watching the mission via drone video footage and was excited to see how well it was going. He decided that rather than flying home, we should stay in the village for a while and clear every single building. This was not a contingency we had planned or prepared for, and the news was deflating. The grumbling began almost immediately. The boys knew this would take all night, and it did.

We finally finished clearing the village in the glow of predawn. By then, it was too late for the helicopters to come and pick us up, because while the 160th Special Operations Aviation Brigade is the very best in the business, they only fly at night. We were effectively stranded, and the Taliban knew it.

As the sun came up, we started to see the town's few remaining citizens fleeing for the hills and open desert. They weren't sticking around for what was about to happen.

The chatter started coming over the radios as the Taliban began to encircle us. We all raced to establish defensive fighting positions inside buildings and across a series of rooftops. Our Tactical Air Controllers started requesting air support to come overhead. This was the Alamo, and if the Taliban wanted a piece of us, they were going to have to come and take it.

We all waited, bleary-eyed and exhausted from the night before. Nobody had brought enough water to be on the ground for a full day, or any food at all. These were not the ideal conditions to find ourselves in a gunfight, but we suspected one was imminent. At last, the silence broke as a volley of rocket-propelled grenades came screaming across the poppy fields. All of them either fell short or skipped into the walls of the mud huts we were occupying. Within seconds, our guys were returning fire to suppress the enemy attack.

This long-range exchange went on for hours as the Taliban attempted one route after another to try and penetrate our defense and overrun us. A continuous stream of aircraft streaked overhead, making gun runs and dropping bombs on enemy positions. By early afternoon, things had calmed down enough to try to get us out of there. An awesome group of aircrews from the 101st Airborne Division agreed to come in and give us a ride home.

As we ran for the birds in the bright midday sun, I watched each of my teammates closely. They were all dehydrated, starving, filthy, and completely spent—and yet somehow more energized than I'd seen them in weeks. The mood on our ride back to Kandahar was light. The guys joked and told crazy stories about how the day had unfolded from their respective vantage points. It was good to see them smile again, exuding the confidence I had become so accustomed to seeing before that horrible week in February. Together, we faced challenges beyond our imaginations and our capabilities. We were no longer the same people or the same team that had showed up in Afghanistan. We were fewer in numbers and badly damaged, yet somehow, we'd managed to grow into who we needed each other to be. When we needed to most, we persevered.

3

Going Down Isn't Going Backward

BLAYNE SMITH AND BRANDON YOUNG

What got us here, won't get us there.
—*Marshall Goldsmith*

While we hope that you never experience what we did as young men in the war, we trust that you have your own crucibles that have challenged you and are challenging you now. We all have felt at one time or another like the ground has just come out from under us. We all have labored in earnest only to feel disappointed by the outcome. All of us have lost. Some of us have learned.

When it feels like you're going downhill, remember that nothing lasts forever and that going down isn't necessarily going backward. Going down can, in fact, be the preamble to your next great peak, especially when you extend the time horizon and take a broader perspective. Often, we need to go downhill in the name of going forward.

To bring this concept to life, so that we can understand the ups and downs of life and leadership, locate ourselves amid adversity, and grasp the five factors of perseverance, we will provide a helpful metaphor.

THE RIDGELINE OF ADVERSITY

Seeing the larger picture in life helps flatten the mountains and fill in the valleys. It shifts our focus from a single pressing challenge to a life that is full of both setbacks and opportunities. This is important because life—and leadership—is not one big mountaintop or valley, but a series of them and everything between.

Consider a great ridgeline. From any single vantage point, you can see the peaks and valleys, the ups and the downs—yet eventually, the contours across the sky become unclear, obscured by the clouds and the limitations of our sight. Put yourself on the side of one of those mountains, and you can see the trail in front of you, the incline before you, and the decline behind you. You can see the top of that hill up ahead and track the distance on a map to know how far you have until you reach it.

Reaching the summit will be hard, but knowing the distance, time, direction, and goal provides some predictability. Like a marathon, the course is marked, and you know what you've signed up for. You must endure the climb to get to the mountaintop (the finish line, the objective). Once you've reached the top, you can see the peaks and valleys around you, but they are not *your* ups and downs. *Your* event is complete. Snap a selfie, crack a beer, and head back to the car. Well done! You've endured a tough hike up the mountain.

In the longer arc of life and leadership, the top of the mountain reveals the rest of the ridgeline laid out before us, with all the ups and downs ahead and many more that we cannot see. We don't get to crack a beer and head to the car after our hilltop selfies. We don't get to opt out (though arguably some do), because there is no car at the trailhead of life. Life and leadership require us to keep moving forward. We can never go back, as much as we may want to. And it's important to understand that valleys, climbs, and rockslides are on that same ridgeline between mountaintops. This is what leadership is actually like. This is what organizations actually experience in a complex world.

We call this *the ridgeline of adversity* and illustrate it this way:

Life is like a ridgeline. It has ups and downs, peaks and valleys, and extends far into the unknown. Throughout our respective journeys, we eventually experience everything the ridgeline has to offer, with all of its rockslides, mountaintops, valleys, and climbs. As we illustrate each of the four positions in which we commonly find ourselves along the ridgeline, consider where you might be at this very moment on your own ridgeline of adversity.

The Rockslide

The rockslide is when everything feels unstable, like the ground has just given way beneath our feet. These are abrupt and unexpected changes that catch us off guard. A rockslide can come in many forms. It may be the loss of a loved one, a big round of layoffs, or the resignation of a key team member.

As leaders, our role is to stop the slide and stabilize. We best do this by shrinking the world down to what we can control and making the next best decision we can. After that, we continue making one good decision at a time until we can clearly assess the situation and move forward. Rockslide moments will always come, and it's important to understand that they are not the time to make large decisions that will be realized years into the future, for two key reasons. First, the organization might not be there tomorrow if conditions don't get under control today. Second, rockslides tend to lead to panicked or reactive thinking, which is not how we want to make big, sweeping decisions. Reactive decisions are often ill thought out and lead to more setbacks. What we want to do is get ourselves on solid footing so that we can take a breath and respond thoughtfully.

Leading our teams out of the rockslide requires understanding what is critical versus what is not. We tend to get stuck debating factors that might not enhance the progress we aim for. A good place to start is by establishing some priorities. First, determine what is truly important versus what is merely interesting. Though a task or project might be interesting, if it doesn't directly get you out of the rockslide or explicitly lead to mission success, it is likely not a priority. You must deprioritize it so you and your team can focus on what you must do to stabilize yourselves.

Once you identify the important projects, personnel, or equipment, the next task is prioritizing their order of focus. Eisenhower put it best in his famous four-box decision matrix that assesses a matter's importance and urgency. If it's urgent and important, do it now. If it's not urgent but important, decide on a time to do it later. If it's urgent but not important, delegate it. And last, if it is neither important nor urgent, delete it.

Adapted from Stephen R. Covey, *The 7 Habits of Highly Effective People* (New York: Simon & Schuster, 1989), 162.

The Mountaintop

We reach the mountaintop when we hit goals. We've worked hard, established priorities, managed setbacks, and reached the top. The mountaintop is a beautiful place that represents achievement. Celebrate every one of them. Embrace those wins and ensure that your teammates do as well. Failing to celebrate a win sets a precedent that nothing is ever good enough—so there's no need to even try. Failing to recognize success is a recipe for complacency. Leaders who subscribe to the "never enough" approach will find themselves overburdened and alone when they hit their mountaintops.

The mountaintop, for all its glory, can be a tricky place to operate from because it can bait us into resting on our laurels. We should take some time to enjoy the view and appreciate how far we've come, but ultimately, we need to keep moving forward. This can be difficult because going forward may require us to descend and give up a little altitude. We may need to revisit or retool some of the things that helped us reach the mountaintop. We might feel like we are taking a step or two back in order to progress—not typically what we want to do. The critical thing to remember here is that *going down isn't going backward!* There will be times when we need to go downhill in the service of going forward.

The key to success on the mountaintop is recognizing that complacency kills. We've all seen a professional sports team jump out to a big lead and then get tight as they start playing not to lose. This rarely works out well. We never win in life by simply clinging to what we have. We succeed long term through a willingness to keep pressing onward, even if it requires us to give up a little of what we've got right now.

So let's be sure to celebrate the wins, learn from where we've been, take stock of what we have . . . then get back at it. We won't know what the trail has in store for us, but to find out, we need to keep going. As much as we may want to plot a perfect path from one mountaintop to the next, planning out each step along the way, that's just not realistic. At some point, we need to set a course, change our socks, pick up our packs, and head out. There are no answers at the trailhead. Everything we need to know is on the trail.

The Valley

Next is the valley: the low point between objectives, the dark dip between where we are and where we want to be. The valley can be haunting, full of doubt, confusion, and frustration. This is the place where it is easiest to feel lost and hopeless—where it is easiest to quit. Maybe we've been working on a project or a new business for a long time, and it just isn't working out. Perhaps our team has suffered loss after loss, and nothing we try is improving the situation. We know we don't want to be in the valley, but we aren't sure exactly how to get out of it. All paths out require climbing uphill, and we may not feel like we have what it takes to make that climb.

Technically speaking, small valleys are actually called "draws," and draws are features that everyone has to traverse in the SFAS* Star Course or the RASP† Land Navigation Course at Cole Range.

---

* Special Forces Assessment and Selection.

† Ranger Assessment and Selection Program.

The task in land navigation is simple yet hard: find "stop signs" in the forest. These points are marked by little orange and white metal signs on a pole. Candidates are given a map, compass, and protractor to plot and find them. And every course contains at least one route of approach that takes candidates through a draw. The draw is typically filled with tangle vines and brush. That foliage stops progress, changes the direction of travel, and frustrates the hell out of you!

Thousands of Ranger and Green Beret hopefuls have found themselves stuck in the draw on the land navigation course and had to decide at that moment how to respond. Some gather their wits and get back on course, while others decide that being a Green Beret or a Ranger isn't for them. Understand this right now: *there are no life epiphanies in the draw, only exit doors.* You can determine if something is right for you after you've worked your way through the draw. You can determine if a direction or an initiative is right for your organization after you've worked through the valley. Making life and strategic decisions in the valley, more often than not, leads to quitting on yourself and your team. Don't take the bait in the valley. Fight through the darkness. Don't quit.

When situations are at their darkest and we are not sure which way to go, the best thing to do is to orient ourselves on something we know, like our mission, and point ourselves in that direction. Just start moving toward something that is true. No hardship will last forever. Orienting your focus from the present moment to a better future is an appropriate step in the valley. Pick your mountaintop and set your teams' eyes on it. Establishing a plan rooted in your organization's core competencies is a critical approach to moving out of the valley. Now is not the time to get lost in innovation. Consider what your team was built to perform and execute it to precision. Identify what is no longer serving the organization in the valley and leave it behind. Like dead weight in a rucksack, those tasks, projects, or wild ideas might need to go for now. It can be hard for anyone to look up when buried under the weight of the nonessential. Sadly, this process can include letting go of people. No caring leader enjoys this process, but in life and leadership, there are times when it makes sense to part ways with partners, vendors, and teammates who are no longer a good fit for the mission.

The Climb

This brings us to the climb, a position that represents the long march toward our goals. The climb occurs when we set an objective, create a strategy, align the team to achieve it, and execute accordingly. This is where leaders must be patient—stay the course, monitor progress, and check for exhaustion or signs of drift. Very little is more frustrating to a team in the climb than a leader who constantly changes priorities and objectives. There is always room to shift an approach that remains in service to the goal. After all, no climb looks the same underfoot as it does on a map, and plans only take you so far. Mike Tyson put it best when he said, "Everyone has a plan until they get punched in the mouth." But shifting *how* we achieve our goals is different from changing *what* our goals are. Here is where we want to make adjustments that keep us moving in the same general direction, small changes along the course that help us progress toward the same mountaintop. The situation may require us to adjust how we get there, but the destination remains intact. Be cautious about the difference between a pivot and change:

Pivot: shifting an approach to achieving a goal when confronted with an obstacle

Change: switching the goal when confronted with an obstacle

The climb is where endurance is very useful. We can put our heads down and continue grinding it out. If we are moving in the right direction and we're making progress toward our goals, sometimes the only thing to do is just keep going. And while that sounds simple, it is rarely easy, because going uphill is hard. It's natural to get halfway through a climb and start to wonder when the hill won't be so steep or if we'll ever get to the top. In these moments, we might start looking for some kind of shortcut to the summit.

Leading a team through the climb requires acknowledging that the same conditions do not equal the same experiences for our people. Exhaustion, frustration, and anxiety will seep in during the climb at different intervals and degrees of severity across the team. Leaders must monitor this and create checkpoints to assess progress and relieve pressure. Extending the metaphor, climbers often use anchors to tie their safety ropes to the wall, lean back, and shake out their arms. As they do this, they remain tied to the rest of the climbers, ensuring no one falls. This is where "never leave a fallen comrade" applies. Teammates will get exhausted and frustrated in the climb. This is normal. Leaders can create these "anchor" moments of reprieve and reflection to reenergize teammates who may be running low on motivation. These moments also mark progress and the path up the mountain. Leaders help their teams by showing the path ahead; reflecting on how far the team has come; and pausing long enough to allow the entire team to rest, regroup, and move forward together. Finding these anchors along the way is critical to getting through a long climb together.

———

Regardless of which position we find ourselves in, we must acknowledge that while life will always be a series of ups and downs, there is only one direction to go: forward. Leading a team along the ridgeline challenges us to manage our own doubts and frustrations while guiding others through theirs and keeping the team together through shared hardship. And regardless of what team we're on or what path we're taking, there will be adversity. Fooling ourselves into thinking otherwise is a dangerous form of self-deception that will leave us unprepared and ill-equipped to deal with the real adversity when it comes. As we've stated, nobody goes undefeated in life, and while we never plan for things to go terribly wrong, eventually they will.

Adversity shakes our core because it triggers fear and anxiety. These are normal responses to abnormal circumstances. The human brain craves patterns and certainty. Patterns emerge in life through routine. We get up, make coffee, start our day, go to work, work out, eat, and so on. We often have dinner at the same time (or try to), frequent the same restaurants, drink the same beverages, and listen to the same artists. It gives us comfort in an otherwise unpredictable world. But adversity invokes fear by cracking a hole through the veneer of certainty that our patterns create. Though we will unpack this in later chapters, understanding that a lack of certainty creates fear is a critical step in overcoming it.

Fear is an uncomfortable word for a lot of people, but it is just a core human emotion, like joy or anger. It is fear that underlies our discomfort or anxiety when life becomes uncertain. Fear of failure. Fear of harm. Fear of harming another. Fear of loss. Fear is a natural response that is neither good nor bad in and of itself. In fact, it is far more good than bad, since fear helps us survive. A healthy fear of a dark alley when walking alone at night can keep us under the street-lights. A healthy fear of dangerous roads in Afghanistan can keep us moving on them under the cover of darkness. Acknowledging fear can help us survive. Confronting fear enables us to thrive. Though it is to be respected, fear can be a killer when not properly engaged. Fear improperly handled can sabotage organizations.

Fear can arrest us and act like a sort of friction that holds us in place. We may choose to put off a difficult decision or delay confronting a hard truth for as long as we can. But we'll eventually have to move, and the driving force behind that movement will likely be *purpose* or *pain*. Having a clear purpose gives us something to run to, a guiding light to point us toward our goals and aspirations. When we run *toward* our purpose, we have the energy and ability to choose the harder, right path that keeps us gradually moving to higher ground on our way to the summit. Conversely, if we let the discomfort build for too long, the pain will cause us to finally move, wanting to be anywhere but here. When we run *from* our pain, we tend to seek comfort through the path of least resistance, moving us gradually downhill into the swamps of avoidance. We get to choose: summit or swamp? We illustrate it this way.

The path of least resistance is, in fact, a subtle form of avoidance. This concept is used in many military contexts. It can help you gain the element of surprise in close-quarter battles, but it can also get you ambushed while patrolling enemy terrain. The path of least resistance in the woods is called a natural line of drift. It's how water flows downhill and how animals create game trails.

For humans reacting out of discomfort, those natural lines of drift are the small concessions we make, the things that we know are wrong but hope won't come back to bite us. It is when we cut that employee who is not upholding performance standards some slack because it's easier than having a difficult conversation. It's when we let a large customer change the agreement without additional payment because it's easier not to upset them. We sidestep the challenges between us and our goals to abate our fears. But the fears and the obstacles remain. The path of least resistance will continue to be a comfortable form of avoidance that will push us further off course and away from our goals. Know this: *nobody drifts into achievement.* Nobody. As leaders, we must fight the drift from pain and pursue the path toward purpose.

Purpose enables us to face our challenges because it reminds us why we're facing them in the first place. Purpose calls us to persevere when adversity is at its peak. This is ultimately what the Rangers and the Green Berets lean on when they get stuck in the draw. The fear is the same for everyone. Getting lost in the woods is scary. Getting lost in the woods when you must pass a course to become a Special Operator is a life-shaking terror. Purpose is the only stabilizing factor that can move you through the fear. Instead of quitting, those who become Rangers and Green Berets choose the harder right over the easier wrong. They calm down, gather the best information they can, locate themselves on the map, plot a course, and drive on. They pivot to achieve the goal instead of changing the goal. They choose the summit instead of the swamp.

Every leader reading this can do the same. You don't have to be starving, dehydrated, and lost in a dark forest to feel the fear of adversity. You don't have to be a Ranger or a Green Beret for your career and goals to be on the line. Many of us feel scared and lost when we are struggling to find our way. Many of us are fighting through our mess and getting nowhere. This likely happens because we are trying to endure when instead we need to persevere. We can keep trying to endure amid adversity, pretending that it's hardship, or we can recognize adversity for what it is and persevere, knowing that hope lies on the other side, along with growth and achievement.

If you're reading this book, we trust you've come up against your own brand of adversity, and that you've tried your best to endure. If you're anything like us, you know what it feels like to be stuck or come up short. And we trust that you've occasionally let yourself down by taking the path of least resistance. Trust us as we call you toward the summit of success. Trust your team to respond. Trust the process.

Victory is calling. Let's go.

4

Change: The Enemy Gets a Vote

BLAYNE SMITH AND BRANDON YOUNG

No man ever steps in the same river twice.

—*Heraclitus*

Our brains do something sneaky when we aren't looking. They trick us into believing that *normal* means *changeless*. That's why whenever we experience change, the desire for everything to go back to normal tends to outweigh the opportunity to seize what's in front of us. We write this in a post–COVID-19 world that requires little illustration on this point. When humans are confronted with change, seeking a sense of normalcy is, well . . . normal. We are wired to seek comfort and safety, and we often find them through stability and predictability. We reinforce this with stories of the *good old days*—an imagined past, a time when things were better than they are today.

And while conditions certainly aren't perfect these days, the truth is they weren't perfect in the *good old days* either.

Much of this brain sneakiness comes down to whether current conditions are meeting our expectations, which in turn are simply a natural extension of our experiences. Some people's experiences cast an expectation of how things *should be*. Conversely, for those who have experienced abuse, neglect, or persecution, their experience may tell them to expect the same in the future because *nothing ever changes*. Both are untrue. The truth is that change is normal because life is always moving forward. We are not the same today as we were yesterday. Not a single one of us. Life *is* change, a simple reality that we all would do well to embrace. When we decide to stop acting like life is happening to us and accept that change is just part of the deal, we are already in a much stronger place from which to persevere. We can learn to make peace with change, prepare for it, and respond appropriately when confronted with it.

CHANGE, THE ETERNAL CONSTANT

Wherever you are today, yesterday is not coming back, and neither is *normal*. Things never go back to normal. There's no such thing. We, veterans, know this all too well. From the first moment of any deployment, we're counting down the days until it's over and we can all go home—back to our families, favorite restaurants, and lives—*back to normal*. We know that we've got a job to do and need to stay focused, yet we still can't help but constantly daydream about the warm hugs and cold beer waiting on the other side. If we can just suck it up and get through this, everything is going to be awesome. Unless it isn't.

The problem is that redeployment* from combat is not just one big Budweiser commercial. Don't get us wrong—reuniting with friends and loved ones is wonderful. It's great to eat a delicious meal and sleep in your own bed, especially without the serious threat of being interrupted by mortar fire. Still, redeployment is tricky at best and brutal at worst. It's full of pitfalls you can't or would prefer not to see. We believe that returning from a forced, difficult situation will be great, only to discover that it isn't that simple. What most of us failed to appreciate about redeployment was that *normal* was gone and never coming back. In ways that we hadn't expected, things changed. We had changed. Our families had changed. The world had changed—and we just didn't recognize how much. If we had to do it again, we would do so much differently. But with our military days far behind us, we assumed that most of those hard lessons learned would be filed away as regrets and probably never revisited. COVID-19 changed that.

Quarantine often felt just like a deployment. We were told where we could go, where we couldn't, and what we were supposed to wear. Nobody was quite sure who was in charge. There was danger in venturing *outside the wire* because of an invisible enemy we couldn't pin down or directly confront. We were stuck there for a while, happy to be alive and healthy, frustrated with all the uncertainty, and ready to get it over with. The only big difference with COVID-19 was that we were *all* deployed: spouses, kids, civilians, everybody. And as, little by little, the country started to reopen and reintegrate, businesses, communities, and schools eventually returned to something that looks

---

* That is, returning home from overseas combat deployments.

like but isn't quite normal. Every leader and business we work with has experienced this, but they've all experienced it differently because the same conditions do not equal the same experiences.

Ten people can be exposed to the same circumstances and have ten completely different experiences. No two people had the same *exact* COVID-19 experience because we all came into the situation with different pasts, values, beliefs, and personalities. And our conditions had slight variations. Some people had children; others did not. Some worked from a laptop; others worked with their hands. Some thrived, and some barely survived when confronted with the change, which brought awareness to the danger of blanket policies or protocols. After COVID-19, some people were eager to return to work and school, while others became comfortable working from home. Still others dealt with real challenges as a result of the crisis. While many made it through the pandemic with only minor consequences to their health and livelihood, we must recognize that millions of others suffered greatly, losing loved ones, shuttering businesses, or picking up long-term health issues. Teams experiencing change need leaders who pay close attention to their people and are willing to support them as individuals, because change is a process, not an event.

In the military, we had to plan for a successful redeployment. We couldn't flip a switch and be back up and running. The changes COVID-19 wrought forced us to look at everything from administration and logistics to personal dynamics and products or services. We had to take stock of what we'd learned, just like an After Actions Review after deployment.

Deployments aren't all bad—far from it. Talk to almost any veteran, and they'll tell you how much they enjoyed certain aspects of being *down range*. Maybe it was the heightened sense of purpose, camaraderie, or simplicity. The same goes for COVID-19. As scary and sad as it was, the pandemic wasn't an entirely negative experience. Many leaders confronted some critical issues during that time, because a crisis tends to put a microscope on pre-existing problems rather than create new ones. COVID-19 did that for a lot of organizations. Many companies, ours included, are stronger today because we persevered through the pandemic. And many others collapsed under adversity. The organizations that persevered accepted that the world had changed and dealt with it. They assessed the situation, made adjustments, and executed them in response. To be sure, things did not go smoothly for most. Along with the loved ones lost and the havoc absorbed by healthcare workers, we all had our plans frustrated and our hopes dashed many times over. But those who rolled with the changes fared well, and those who railed against them did not. Nobody plans to fail, and nobody planned on a pandemic, but the lesson here is not to give up on planning. Quite the contrary; the lesson is to remember *why* we plan in the first place.

PREPARING FOR CHANGE

President Dwight Eisenhower said, "Plans are worthless, but planning is everything."[1] At some point, all plans become worthless because nothing ever goes as planned. Things change. But planning is everything because it prepares our people for what is to come and aligns them to a clear goal. Preparation and alignment are critical because "no plan survives first contact with the enemy."[2] Warfighters know this because, just like life, war *is* change. It is unpredictable and disorienting; it shatters expectations. It takes one mission to experience this truth. After that, unpredictability is a lifestyle.

We thought we knew what war would look and feel like as young soldiers, but our dreams of "The Show" turned out to be no dreams at all. In war, things rarely go as planned. We can do all the right things, everything that our planning told us to do, and bad things will still happen because *the enemy gets a vote*. But preparation allows us to cast the final vote. A common mistake we make in leadership is falling in love with our plans and predictions. Prediction invites fragility and makes our plans precious, vulnerable to even small deviations. Unforeseen events can shake us to our core. In moments like these, we truly realize how little control we have in life and that even the most detailed plans can't protect us from every possible contingency. We do not plan in order to predict what will happen in the future; we plan in order to prepare for the future we cannot predict.

Those who spend the most time predicting the future often show up as the least prepared. Plans shouldn't tell us what to expect; they should prepare us for the unexpected. RASP and SFAS are great laboratories for this. It's the guys in the barracks talking about what they heard RASP's Cole Range is like or how many points to expect on the land navigation course who quit the moment their predictions are dispelled. Or the guys who find themselves 10 km into the SFAS Star Course, stuck in a draw. They discover that it isn't what they expected it to be or is harder than planned. And that's the moment all of their predictions fall apart. It's worth stating again: *there are no life epiphanies in the draw, only exit doors*. To be clear, taking the exit door is quitting. The first time you quit will be the hardest; it will only get easier every time after that.

The successful guys are the ones who prepared. You could always sense the calm energy of those who'd prepared themselves to handle whatever came their way, the ones who trained their bodies for the hardship and their minds for the adversity of selection. It was a totally different energy from those who were always looking for inside information about what was coming next, hoping to gain some small advantage and avoid being caught off guard. The predictors talked to everyone and their mother about what selection is like, in search of the cheat codes. By the way, the people who are always happy to share the cheat codes are usually the ones who tried and failed selection. In the Army we call those people "barracks lawyers." It never made sense to us why people would listen to a word they said about a course they failed. Conversely, the guys who passed the course were the ones that took it one step at a time and just did their best on every task until it was over. Their advice usually sounded something like, "Show up ready and don't quit." When change inevitably strikes, preparation enables us to work decisively through setbacks, navigate the terrain (not the plan), and follow through with action over intentions.

Working decisively through setbacks means making one good decision at a time based on the situation. Decisive doesn't mean certain. Decisive means confident. This is a critical distinction—that we can absolutely have confidence without having certainty. Confidence in our decisions comes from seeing the situation clearly, taking in the information at hand, considering the options, and choosing the wisest approach to achieve the best possible outcome.

We launched Applied Leadership Partners at the beginning of March 2020. With three client engagements already on the books, we were poised for a strong start. Three days later—when the world shut down—we had none. Needless to say, we were concerned about the viability of our new business. In those early, unpredictable days of the pandemic, we decided that we needed to simply respect the moment and be generous. And while we were not certain we would succeed, we were confident in ourselves and immediately pivoted to online operations in order to achieve the goal: help leaders be more effective and sustainable.

Fortunately, we were already quite comfortable with virtual operations, having led a distributed workforce in more than 200 cities (we were Zooming before Zoom was cool). We knew we had insights to offer the world as we found ourselves on the sidelines of a crisis instead of on the front lines. We decided that though we couldn't do everything we wanted to do, we would do everything that we could do. We wrote a lot about leadership, shared generously, and hosted 60-minute coaching calls for free! We advised teachers, healthcare providers, insurance agents, moms, government employees, and many others who took us up on our offer. We didn't know how it would turn out, but by the fall of 2020, we had started booking partnerships and our business was off and running. We had sharpened our virtual presenting skills and developed a lot of great content, which made us valuable to many organizations that were wrestling with remote and hybrid work settings. Most importantly, we consistently reminded each other of two critical promises we made to ourselves and our families: (1) we bet on ourselves, and (2) we walk in faith.

Preparation creates that shared consciousness that General Stan McChrystal speaks about in *Team of Teams*. It does not create a script for everyone to follow. Scripts don't work in real life. They work in movies and shows because those are artful illustrations of reality, but in actual reality, we will experience setbacks. There's no one waiting to yell, "Cut!" and reset the scene. Supply chain issues will delay the production and delivery of goods. Travel bans will disrupt our ability to get face to face with those we serve. Rate increases will slow buyer patterns and challenge sales goals. And employee fear will prevent some from feeling safe in office work environments. Preparation allows leaders to adjust accordingly to ensure mission success, particularly when teammates share and create goals during the planning process.

Navigating the terrain, not the plan, comes from goal clarity and team alignment. Every team member and employee should be able to answer two questions: (1) *Why are we doing this?* and (2) *What do you want me to do?* All of them.

Why are we doing this? Vision is a critical force multiplier for all teams. A clear vision casts a vivid image of a new future. It is the very purpose our work aims to achieve. A prepared team can be identified by the whole team's ability to articulate the purpose of their work—from the commander to the lowest Private, from the CEO to the janitor. In the military, we use a statement called the commander's intent. It casts a clear understanding of what must be achieved and why. When we were leading a national veteran-serving nonprofit called Team Red, White, and Blue, we intended to enrich the lives of America's veterans by connecting them to their community through physical and social activity. We didn't mind exactly how the 2,000 leaders in 212 cities connected the 150,000 veterans and community members. We just cared that they did. Some surfed, some ran, some did yoga, some did CrossFit workouts, and some had coffee. What mattered was they did it together, resulting in 50,000 events per year.

What mattered was that they knew the vision and what they needed to do to achieve it.

What do you need me to do to accomplish our goals? Every team member should be able to answer this question in order to navigate the terrain, not the plan. It doesn't have to be overly complicated. We used simple terms in the military to communicate this: task and purpose. Task: what you need to do. Purpose: why we need you to do it. For example, task: run the IT department; purpose: so we can communicate with each other and our customers and securely protect our data. Deeper formulations of this emerged when appropriate, like defining the conditions the person was operating in or the standards expected, but in the end, the task was clear, and that's the point. From top to bottom and side to side (in flatter organizations), communicating what is expected and why it is expected creates a more adaptable team. It also creates what we in the military call nesting. Nesting helps interdisciplinary teams understand how each helps the other and how all efforts impact the whole.

Growth doesn't come from good intentions; it comes through good follow-through. The task is clear on the land navigation course for RASP. Task: Find four points in the woods by plotting five points correctly, creating a plan, and navigating the terrain, and then return within four hours. You have a map, a compass, and a protractor. You are forbidden to speak to anyone on the course or use any GPS device for aid. Purpose: To see how you handle setbacks; navigate the terrain (not the plan); and follow through when you are scared, lost, tired, and hungry. To see if you can think on your feet when it's hard and achieve your objective, regardless of the setbacks. If you cannot do these things, you are not who we are looking for to serve at the tip of the spear. It's not a knock against you, and it's not personal. This is what is required of a Special Operator. And this is where we see who walks the talk. Everybody wants to be a Ranger . . . until they have to do Ranger shit.

It's easy to fall in love with what you think something will be like and then get shattered when confronted with reality. We all think we know what marriage or having a baby will be like until we get married or have a baby. It's all pregnancy photos, dandelion fields, and belly kisses until you're up at 3 AM soothing a colicky baby while your partner pretends to sleep. These unrealistic expectations are precisely the predictions that make follow-through very hard. Marriage is hard. But marriage is worth it. Parenting is hard. But parenting is worth it. The SFAS Star Course is hard too. It's supposed to be. And you better believe being a Green Beret is harder! In war, in business, or in life, we have to get out of our heads and get into reality.

We'll tell you a secret about land navigation in the SOF community. When you get your points, you make a plan. You take your time on the front end and plot your points. You check them and recheck them. You make a plan. You plot azimuths between them and conduct a map reconnaissance for handrails, checkpoints, and backstops. And when all that is said and done, you get up and get to it, because all the answers are out there on the course. All of our answers are out on the trail. We can have all of the best intentions at the wedding or the baby shower, but those amount to very little when reality shatters our expectations and changes our plans. We must commit to actions over intentions if we are to expect our teams to persevere through adversity, to respond appropriately to change rather than simply reacting to it.

RESPONDING TO CHANGE

When the bullets start flying in combat, everyone starts looking at the leader, and as the leader goes, so the team goes. Leaders in every industry experience their equivalent—thankfully without the bullets! When confronted with change, we either respond or react. *Responding* to change is a timely, thoughtful, wise adjustment to accomplish goals. *Reacting* is immediate, reflexive, and often emotional. Sometimes, goals get achieved when we react, but usually with some collateral damage. Often they do not, though the collateral damage remains. It doesn't take a rockslide to bring about the impulse to react. Routine human interaction within a stressful, uncertain environment will almost always bring about reactivity.

Fear is at the root of all reactions under stress. Biologically, the limbic system triggers the sympathetic nervous system, leading to a fight-or-flight response. When the sympathetic nervous system comes online, the prefrontal cortex goes offline. Our prefrontal cortex regulates thought, emotions, and actions. Fight or flight disengages it. It can be nearly impossible to respond calmly when we are frightened and the sympathetic nervous system is in charge. This is why so many veterans struggle to regulate emotions postwar. Post-traumatic stress disorder (PTSD) hijacks the limbic system and tricks the brain into constantly interpreting the need to fight or flee from our surroundings. To respond instead of reacting, the parasympathetic nervous system must be activated to calm us down and bring our higher faculties back online. The ability to respond allows us to consider the setback and the situation while offering the opportunity to determine the next best step that will lead to success. Responding is far more effective than reacting. Leaders can choose responding by creating space between their emotions and the situation, setting the tone for the team, and thoughtfully dealing with the situation.

Creating space between our emotions and the situation is critical. In a situation where we have no space, we must create space. In Special Forces training, what they are primarily trying to assess and teach is your ability to have a thoughtful, appropriate response to a high-stress, intentionally ambiguous situation. Often, you have to choose between two bad options, forcing you to pick a course of action that's *the least bad.* When you're a person who is used to solving problems, having to choose between a host of bad options is very stressful. The cadre wants to see if you're going to shut down at that moment, telling them you're not the kind of leader that will thrive in the Special Operations environment. It doesn't seem fair at the time, but it makes perfect sense because they are teaching you how to activate the parasympathetic nervous system and use your higher faculties. Candidates learn a tool during the course to help them understand that they have more time than they think when making a decision. The tool is *LTPR,* an acronym for *listen, think, pause,* and *respond.*

- *Listen* to who is speaking, what they are saying, and the environment. Listening seems like a lost art in a time when it feels like everyone is just talking. In our advising, we practice something called *listening for distance*—simply letting a person speak until they are done speaking. We allow another person to own the airtime and our undivided attention. It can be tough because most of us are uncomfortable with silence and want to solve problems. Rather than truly listening, we are inclined to fill the space and get ahead of ourselves. We miss important details because we think about our responses rather than listen. But when we listen, we are far more apt to pick up the subtleties of the situation. Especially when we listen with our eyes. In *You're Not Listening*, Kate Murphy points out that Wernicke's area—where the brain processes speech—is located at the juncture of the visual and auditory cortices. That is why lipreading accounts for 20% of your comprehension of a perfectly audible conversation, while 55% of the emotional content of a message is communicated nonverbally.[3] Effective listening allows us to gain clarity and consider the next step.

- *Think!* Think before you act. Consider what's happening, what you heard, what you observed, and what you might say or do next. We often tell people to consider the impact of what comes next, which is why the next move is to pause.

- *Pause.* Right before you are about to speak, don't. Pausing can feel like an eternity in a stressful situation, but it's so important. Take a breath. Take a few breaths—deep ones. Say what you're about to say in your mind and gauge whether it has sharp edges. Consider how to say it in those moments; sometimes, you'll even find that the person will continue to talk, and you will collect more important information to inform your response further.

- Then, *respond.* And when you do respond, do it clearly and succinctly, setting the tone for the team.

Cool breeds cool. And panic breeds panic. When stress strikes, team members focus on leaders—and leaders must handle this well.

It's part of the job. Team members will watch what the leader does and then follow accordingly. Humans naturally mirror others. Watch how a baby reacts to someone making faces at them. Cry, and the baby cries. Smile, and the baby smiles. It's reflexive and signals the power of human connection. When change strikes, if we can slow down and respond, the team will see that as the normal behavior pattern and follow suit. If the sky is always falling, though, you can believe the team will be running for cover. Even though change is stressful, our modeling can release pressure for the team, regardless of your situation. During CQB,* for instance, you're blowing doors off hinges, shotgunning doorknobs, chucking bangers,† and clearing rooms. It's fast and furious. It is intense. So at times, leaders call for a "pressure check." One by one, every man checks ammo, replaces a mag, and takes a deep breath. These techniques aren't just for Special Operators; they can be learned, practiced, and used effectively by anybody in any circumstance.

Getting some space between our emotions and the circumstances is also essential. Differentiation of self, a practice from family systems therapy, is a useful framework for leaders. On an axis representing two extremes, with detachment on one side and enmeshment on the other, differentiation is the central, golden mean. *Detachment* is complete disengagement. It's like looking at someone in a hole and saying, "Hate it for ya!" Disengaged leaders relay apathy to their teammates.

---

* Close Quarters Battle.

† Flash-bang grenades that disorient enemy combatants.

Enmeshment is an overidentification with the problem. It's a feeling that you also have to jump in the hole because somebody else is down there. Enmeshment affects clarity, judgment, and effectiveness. Differentiation enables effectiveness. Author Steve Cuss's work in *Managing Leadership Anxiety* is helpful here. He says that differentiation is "the courage to lead people to a difficult place while still being deeply connected."[4] A differentiated leader sees the situation clearly, cares for the people involved deeply, and manages the tension for maximum effectiveness without being emotionally or logically compromised. Managing that tension can be difficult, but it is critically important.

With perseverance being a long game, it's common to hit the wall occasionally. Psychologically, hitting the wall feels like a wet blanket on the soul or running in mud. Sometimes, it feels like we just can't will our brains to work correctly even though we know what needs to be done. We all experience this. Being around the same people, in the same place, with what feels like a no-win situation for a long time can lead to feelings of helplessness. What happens next is personality driven. Some get depressed and shut down, while others get anxious and cry. Still others emotionally withdraw and seethe with anger. We express this in many ways, but when we hit the wall, we must take action.

A helpful cognitive behavioral therapy tool for this is called *stop–breathe–refocus.*

- *Stop!* Speak the word out loud. Our brains get stuck in thinking patterns of rumination—worry, doubt, anger, and frustration—that originate with anxiety. When we say "Stop!", we pull out of the repeating loop in our minds.

- *Breathe.* Take a few minutes for some intentional belly breathing (are you starting to see how vital breathing is?). Take it all in, filling the bottom of your lungs first, and then exhale. Breathing is that rare biological function that can be done both unconsciously and consciously. When we breathe consciously or purposefully, we activate our parasympathetic nervous system, which lets our mind and body know that we neither need to fight nor flee.

- Last, *refocus.* What are you mentally fixating on now, and how is it helping relieve your frustration? If it's not, you need to refocus on something else.

Once we get out of reactivity, we must constantly work to stay in a response posture. And remember, leaders, we aren't the only ones stressed out. When change hits, everyone loses their sense of normalcy. Reassuring others that you are feeling disrupted while reassuring them of your care for them makes a difference. When change thrusts us into positions we cannot escape—like being forward-deployed to a firebase on the Afghanistan–Pakistan border, stuck in a loveless marriage, or locked down by a global pandemic—running for the exit is not the move. Perseverance is. The first step to perseverance is recognizing that change brings about a great deal of uncertainty. The next is dealing with the uncertainty that change creates.

5

Uncertainty: The Unknown Distance March

BLAYNE SMITH AND BRANDON YOUNG

The oldest and strongest emotion of mankind is fear,
and the oldest and strongest kind of fear is fear of
the unknown.
—*H. P. Lovecraft*

Uncertainty is scary. It feels like being alone in the woods at night with a flashlight. You're at a fork in the path, unsure of which way to go. You shine the flashlight down each trail but can only see as far as the light allows. The woods rustle around you, and your chest tightens. Unable to decide, you wish to see just a little farther down the trail. If you could only sit down and build a better flashlight!

One that could illuminate more of the darkness before you. But you cannot. The light will only go this far, and lingering only diminishes the range as the batteries die. Alternatively, you can pick a path and take a step forward, which will allow you to see one step farther into the darkness.

If we move to the edge of the light, we can see the path will emerge one step of courage at a time. If the path seems right, we take another step. If not, we can go back. It doesn't have to be fatalistic, and it never is certain. That simple (yet difficult) act of courage unglues our feet, frozen by the fear of uncertainty. Life is change, and change is uncertain. Moving or failing to move is a choice either way. We either choose to act or let the situation act upon us. We either let the light illuminate the path or let it dim while we wait.

We see this in various contexts. No one is ready for a baby until they walk out of the hospital with their baby. No one is ready to start a business until they are months into running their business. And no one learns to lead through uncertainty by sitting down on the dark trail while trying to build a better flashlight. So, stop trying to build a better flashlight. Instead, build a team ready for the challenges of the real world with all its dark trails and limited lighting. Build a team prepared for uncertainty.

Uncertainty comes from being confronted with situations outside our training, experience, expectations, and plans. Humans crave certainty; we seek it as a constant attempt to find a degree of stasis in our surroundings. We want to know what's ahead. And even though certainty truly is a fallacy in life, we still figure out ways to settle into comfort zones. Change shakes that false sense of certainty, creating fear. This is when the team needs leaders the most, and when leaders earn their salt. In the face of uncertainty, leaders must focus on the mission, manage fears, and lead people through adversity.

THE MISSION > THE MOMENT

We often tell our partners, "You cannot manage your way out of leadership." We sometimes describe management as all the things we need to do in order to keep the team working properly, while leadership is what we need to do when things are *not* working properly. Uncertainty requires leadership. Many organizations operate with very well-defined processes and procedures that enable them to function well. Often, these patterns solidify into standard operating procedures, or SOPs. These checklists and flowcharts help a team to consistently and safely deliver their products and services to customers and end users. The unquestionably valuable norms in these SOPs allow companies to run by providing pathways of certainty in an otherwise uncertain world. But try as you might, you simply cannot plan for and chart out every possible scenario. There are always exceptions to the rule, especially when adversity strikes.

The moment is that experience brought about by change that exposes our fragility and produces fear. Moments occur when there seems to be no discernable path toward achieving our goals (especially by working our SOPs) and no foreseeable end. And while the type of adversity may be unique to a particular situation, the moments of fearful uncertainty are ubiquitous. Moments like a bank run that thrusts an entire industry into chaos (as seen with Silicon Valley Bank in 2023). Moments like an all-star medical diagnostics company getting acquired by the largest healthcare conglomerate in the world, causing those employees who built that boutique company to fear the inevitability of consolidation and reorganization. Moments like a hurricane decimating properties held by a hazard insurance company, forcing employees to manage seemingly endless claims and cries for help from those affected. Moments like the COVID-19 lockdowns with no clear end in sight.

Whatever the moment is, it is highlighted by the unknown, and no one likes the unknown. But navigating the unknown lies at the core of the SOF units we grew up in, making us uniquely conditioned to lead through the seemingly endless uncertainty of the 21st century. What we learned in the Rangers and the Green Berets prepared us for the mergers and acquisitions we led through, the upstart non-profit that became the fastest-growing veteran service organization in America, building our own business, leading our families, and beyond. Special Operators are special not because they are the biggest and the strongest but because they are able to excel in the asymmetry, austerity, and adversity that characterizes unconventional warfare. We are hand selected because we are prepared to keep fighting and find a way to win when those moments strike. And we regularly train for the unknown.

One of the most commonly used tests in Special Operations units is the unknown distance ruck march. This simple but diabolical exercise assesses candidates during selection and builds grit and resolve during training. The ruck is often called "the ultimate equalizer." It can make a 250-pound linebacker fall by the wayside while a 140-pound teenager drives on. The ruck does not discriminate, and it does not relent.

The unknown distance march isn't about the weight of the ruck or the number of miles covered. It's about the uncertainty—the ability to persevere through continuous hardship for however long it takes. It's about learning to focus on the mission, not the moment.

Ruck marching is a painful endeavor to begin with, even when you know how far you're traveling. But walking an unknown distance at night over punishing terrain teaches you a lot about yourself and your teammates. The one penetrating thought that seeps into your mind amid the strain and the pain is whether or not you will quit. Will you break when it gets hard, the finish line is nowhere in sight, and you just want it to end? Or will you find the strength to press on, lean on your teammates, and complete the mission? Sadly, many will take a knee on the side of the road and decide not to get back up. Their march is over, and while they get to keep the blisters, they never get to see what's at the top of the hill.

In 2006, Brandon had the privilege of competing in the Best Ranger Competition, and the unknown distance march put a microscope on his resolve and reliance upon his teammate. He shares his experience here.

———

Like the rest of the teams, Jeremiah and I stepped out at "0-Dark-Thirty," and I knew it would be a rough night. Seven years earlier, I had learned an important lesson about myself during Ranger School. You can starve me, you can smoke me, you can load me down with weight, and you can make me walk for days on end. But sleep deprivation is my weakness.

The Best Ranger Competition is like the Ironman on steroids. It's 60 miles in 60 hours with no sleep while you push your limits with common Ranger tasks like shooting, land navigation, parachuting, obstacle courses, and other events. The mission for every competitor standing in their two-man buddy teams at the starting line is simple: cross the finish line. Most do not accomplish this mission.

The march started after the first 20 hours of nonstop competition, and I was exhausted. Though always a strong ruck marcher, I was droning (falling asleep while walking) a few miles in and hallucinating. We had no clue how long the event would last. The only instructions were *Go! Until you're told to stop.* Relying on my teammate, I kept putting one foot in front of the other as he nursed me with packets of electrolytes, sugary drink mixes, candy bars, and encouragement. It was miserable. I just wanted to stop and go to sleep. But I didn't. I wasn't going to let my teammate down.

We lumbered on through the musky Georgia night one footfall at a time. Walk the uphills, run the downhills. Hope began to stir as we passed other teams of Rangers, giving them a thumbs up and a word of encouragement as they dropped behind us two by two. Jeremiah knew just how to awaken me fully: "Hey, let's start counting the bodies we pass and just run our race, B." One team . . . two . . . three . . . four . . . the teams would emerge on the horizon and fall behind us to the road.

Eventually, a storm erupted upon the pines and the asphalt. We dropped the hammer and ran most of the miles after that. When we finally emerged into a clearing and were told to get on the trucks, only two teams had made it in before us. We would go on to place third in the competition, but I never would have seen the finish line without my Ranger Buddy. I never would have finished had I allowed the pain and uncertainty of the moment to overcome my resolve and commitment to the mission. I never would have accomplished the mission had I let the moment overtake me.

––––

Leaders, we will never achieve our missions if we give the moment greater power over us than it deserves. We must recognize a few things about those moments of adversity.

First, nothing lasts forever. Moments of acute hardship and the unknown will come, and they will go. How long they stay is rarely within our control, but holding on to the fact that eventually it will end, is. There's an old saying: "You never quit Ranger School at night." You wait for the light of a new day because the misery of the preceding night will fade once you begin to move again. The same axiom applies to our business ventures. You never quit a product, process, or person at the point of impact—when we are closest to hardship, and when emotions are at their highest. See it through to the light of a new day.

Second, our feelings follow our focus. If we focus on the fear, our feelings will convince us to fight, fly, or freeze. Our feelings lie to us all the time. They bait us into the path of least resistance to avoid discomfort. If we focus on the mission, the purpose we had from the outset, we can view the pain as a necessary part of the process and transcend the moment. We are not advocating for dissociation in this way. We are advocating for perspective. We don't want to ignore our feelings; we want to examine them thoughtfully, understand where they are coming from, and put them in perspective. It's usually helpful to get a second set of eyes on our problems when we're emotional. Another's perspective can be hugely beneficial when we're either too close to a problem or too blind to see it fully.

Last, remember the summit or the swamp in the midst of uncertainty. We get to choose in these moments. Do we take the harder path toward the summit and mission achievement, or will we take the path of least resistance toward the swamp? Because you're reading this book, we trust you're the kind of leader who chooses the mission over the moment. Let's talk about how we do so without losing our minds—or our teams.

MANAGING OUR FEARS

We've argued that the core feeling that uncertainty creates is fear. How that fear manifests depends upon a person's disposition, experiences, and unique circumstances. Fear can present as anxiety, worry, disconnection, anger, or depression—some freeze, some fight, some fly. Regardless of how we experience fear, what matters most is how we respond to it. We get to be afraid—after all, we're human beings. We do not, however, get to allow our fears to run the show—after all, we're leaders. To lead our teams through uncertainty, we must respond well in the face of change by tapping into the resilience we've built before those moments of impact.

Resilience is the key to sustainable effectiveness—particularly in fearful circumstances. Resilience allows us to adapt to the discomfort of fear and uncertainty and lead people to ensure we accomplish our missions. A resilient leader holds the team up instead of letting it down. Building resilience must be done proactively, consistently, and (ideally) before difficult situations occur.

A resilient life is a rich life, consisting of *health*, *people*, and *purpose*. We've worked on these factors for years, particularly in the veteran-serving nonprofit space while leading Team RWB. There, our amazing team enriched the lives of America's veterans by connecting them to their community through physical and social activities. The organization was founded in 2010, during some of the bloodiest years of the war on terror, and while more than 400,000 veterans a year were separating from service and trying to reintegrate into their communities (though 60% were living in counties from which they had not originated). It was tough work, but by the time we left in 2017, we had 150,000 members, 212 chapters, and 2,000 volunteer leaders hosting 50,000 events per year to help veterans increase the richness of their lives to prevent some of the nastiest downstream effects of failed reintegration—like addiction, homelessness, underemployment, isolation, and suicide. Throughout those years, as we worked with the military, veterans, their family members, and civilians, we got *a lot* of reps in at resilience building and did *a lot* of rigorous measurement and evaluation with Dr. Caroline Angel. We published papers, spoke on panels, disrupted the narrative about veterans, and informed people how America cares for them. We distilled our approach down to what we call the Enrichment Equation:

Health + People + Purpose = Rich Life

You don't need to go into academic detail to adopt the Enrichment Equation, but there are some things to focus on that will build your resilience in advance of life's uncertainty.

- *Health:* Health is not optional or nice to have; it is vital. Without health, we are treading water, and the weight of fear will drag us under. With health, we are robust, adaptable, and able to weather the moment and focus on the mission. Health has three main components: physical, mental, and spiritual. *Physical health* is the foundation of our wellness and resilience, greatly influencing our energy, immunity, and mental acuity. Maintaining our physical health includes frequent physical activity, healthy nutrition, and restful sleep. *Mental health* includes mood states, cognitive functioning, and emotional health (inspiration, optimism, gratitude, and open-mindedness), complemented by the positive moral emotions of self-compassion and self-pride. *Spiritual health* includes connecting (with God or a higher power, oneself, others, and the environment), meaning, value, transcendence, and becoming (the growth and progress in life).[5]

- *People:* Humans are not meant to be alone. We all innately need people in our lives. So, investing in relationships is huge—partners, family, friends, mentors, colleagues, kids, and so forth. These investments buoy us when things are hard and give us a sense of belonging. The people category has two main components: genuine relationships and engaged citizenship. *Genuine relationships* include social support and the recognition that a sense of belonging to a larger group is a fundamental human need. Genuine relationships are high-lighted by trusted, positive, and enduring relationships with others. *Engaged citizenship* includes a sense of connection to and responsibility for the communities in which we live and work. It generates caring and a bias for action through help-ing behavior.[6]

- *Purpose:* Knowing what to do in life is less important than knowing why we do it. Purpose arises from being connected to something larger than yourself. A sense of purpose creates hope (a belief that greater things are to come even in times of joy or difficulty). Purpose is critical. Without purpose, we lack hope. Hopelessness breeds helplessness. Helplessness is a sickness that spreads when it goes unchecked. We both felt helpless when our brothers were killed in Afghanistan. We all felt helpless to some extent throughout the COVID-19 pandemic. Purpose pulls us out of that tailspin. Know-ing why we do what we do, and for what intended outcome, is critical.

BARRIERS TO BUILDING RESILIENCE

We all talk about resilience a lot these days. But what are we *really* doing to build it? More often than not, well-intentioned leaders preach wellness without living it. And if you can't live it, you can't give it. In our time with leaders across various industries, we have identified four common barriers to investing in our wellness: poor modeling, identity asymmetry, the seduction of busyness, and the balance fallacy. Let's address these to ensure we clear our obstacles to build resilience and model it for our teammates. Remember, perseverance for leaders is about guiding teams through adversity—not getting through it alone.

Poor modeling is where it all begins. This barrier looks like telling our people to shut it down and take time for themselves while we keep emailing others at eleven o'clock at night and taking calls on vacation. The message and the activity do not line up. We often pair these actions with statements like, "My people know that I do not expect a response from them at that time of night." But the truth is that the behavior models an expectation. At a minimum, our people will think twice about missing that meeting while on PTO or knocking that one task out after dinner instead of spending time with their families. Two great ways to overcome this are to (1) take the time to invest in wellness and (2) make it public within your team. A simple tactic for achieving both goals is to place important, life-enriching tasks, like a workout or picking up a kid from school, on your shared work calendar. Try it. You'll be amazed at how significant an impact such a small tactic can create.

Identity asymmetry is placing a disproportionate amount of our identity in our work. As high performers and career professionals, we commonly identify very closely, if not completely, with our work. This is why, within the first minute of meeting someone, we often ask, "What do you do?" Who you are is more important than what you do. What you do matters and is a part of who you are, but it is not the whole. You matter in many aspects of life—to your family, friends, and community—not just to your profession. To perform better in our professions, we must develop a greater sense of whole life, or it will lack the necessary aspects of richness to prepare us for the hard times when they strike. And they will strike. Far too many of us have bought into the '80s/'90s playbook—getting the money, the success, the car, the spouse, the kids, and the mortgage—only to wake up one day wondering why you feel empty and where the payoff actually is. In those moments, we need to go back and engage with the spouse, the kids, the home, and the community we live in, and we'll find what we were looking for in the first place. Because all of those aspects of our lives were, in truth, just looking for us. None of them cared about the job that enables our lifestyle.

Next is *the seduction of busyness*. We'd all love to find the time to work on our health, our relationships, and our passions, but we can't because we're just too busy. We never rise and shine, only rise and grind. We've come to recognize activities over action as proxies of success in the business world. We see this a lot in sales teams. Most use a customer relationship management platform that tracks the number of opportunities, sales calls, and rates of closed or lost deals. Many sales organizations also track vehicle mileage and number of flights per year. Call volumes matter, but calls for volume's sake do not. Neither do miles for mileage's sake. Activities tend to become status proxies that turn into behavioral patterns. But creating a bias for action, instead of a bias for activity, is required both to be effective and to protect our time in order to live a rich, resilient life. We must focus energy on what makes us effective, not merely busy, by setting appropriate boundaries for email, meetings, calls, and even flights to allow space for deep work and quality time. We cannot remain busy all the time and expect our (or our people's) best. We must create a better way.

The last barrier to wellness is *the balance fallacy*. The term *work–life balance* is ubiquitous in business vocabulary but is a terrible approach to life. Pick your metaphor for balance—they all sound stressful: the ledger, the scale, the tightrope, the balance beam, the balls in the air, and the spinning plates. Balance requires us to manage competing interests delicately. We play a zero-sum game where we're doling out pieces of ourselves. We become compartmentalized, with X% going to one and Y% going to another. But we'd rather be 100% us at all times and avoid the pain of constantly having to shift gears. Living an integrated or harmonious life is a far superior alternative. An integrated life is far more like a pizza than a pie chart, where we divide up percentages of our time and hope that our attention matches. Let's be honest: If all the ingredients of a pizza were portioned out like a pie chart, it would be a terrible pizza.

Integration respects the whole of who we are and what we bring to the table. It recognizes that we are professionals, leaders, parents, spouses, friends, athletes, and so on in all aspects of our lives. Recognizing our responsibility as parents *and* business leaders actually increases our effectiveness. It does not diminish it. It also makes room for leadership in the real world with all its demands upon our time and attention. We still will have hard deadlines. We will face competing interests, which we can approach in a thoughtful, integrated manner that enables trade-offs without blowoffs or blowouts. Remember that real success is the ability to do great work, consistently, over the long haul. We definitely will need to surge now and again or just push through a hard patch, but that should be the exception and not the rule. Get ahead of this stuff as best you can!

We harp on wellness as a prophylactic form of resilience because our capacity to lead in uncertainty depends on it. The team suffers if we lack any margin because we are already physically and emotionally frayed. The team suffers if we lack genuine relationships that we can lean on amid the strain of uncertainty. The team suffers if we cannot perceive a clear sense of purpose for why we must persevere when times are hard. And when the team suffers, the mission is immediately at risk. We can do better. To persevere when uncertainty strikes, we must get "left of bang."

Getting left of bang means building up our capacity for resilience and preparing for the fearful moments (the "bang") before they happen. It's building our competencies to *stop-breathe-refocus* and *LTPR* before real adversity strikes. We have shared this traditional warfighter insight with leaders in various industries to help them understand what the Greek poet Archilochus meant when he wrote, "We don't rise to the level of our expectations; we fall to the level of our training."

Consider the managers who constantly put out fires on the team. What happens when that leader is overextended and a critical teammate calls out sick, or the supply chain inhibits production goals for the day, or the market takes another unexpected downturn, or the big client notifies them that they are moving to a competitor? The likelihood of overcoming this kind of stressful moment is significantly diminished without a bank of physical, emotional, and spiritual energy to draw from; without the ability to call upon another for support; and without the ability to see a path of hope through the frustration, anger, and fear.

This is so important that we would like you to take a moment and consider where you are at and where you'd like to be, as it relates to these factors. Once you've done that for *you*, we'll discuss how we can lead *others* through the uncertainty.

Let's start by taking a simple inventory of where you are right now. On a scale of 1–10, rate where you think you are regarding the following factors and briefly describe why.

```
1                          5                          10
|--------------------------|--------------------------|
POOR                   AVERAGE                 EXCELLENT
```

CATEGORY	SCORE	DESCRIPTION
Physical Health		
Mental Health		
Spiritual Health		
Genuine Relationships		
Engaged Citizenship		
Sense of Purpose		

Note: As you complete this exercise, be honest and give yourself some grace—we all have opportunities to improve. Also, how we rate ourselves changes as time goes on, so consider rechecking every 90 days.

Now, consider one area in each category that could be strengthened or started, and create a plan for it. Focus on one simple goal and three concrete tactics for each one.

UNCERTAINTY: THE UNKNOWN DISTANCE MARCH

FACTOR	GOAL	TACTICS	HOW WILL YOU KNOW YOU ARE SUCCESSFUL?	WHO CAN HELP YOU STAY ON TRACK?	HOW WILL YOU CELE-BRATE YOUR SUCCESSES?
Physical Health		1. 2. 3.			
Mental Health		1. 2. 3.			
Spiritual Health		1. 2. 3.			
Genuine Relation-ships		1. 2. 3.			
Engaged Citizenship		1. 2. 3.			
Sense of Purpose		1. 2. 3.			

Example: Physical Health

Goal: Walk at least 5,000 steps per day (5 days/week)

Tactics: 1. Start my day with a walk. 2. Schedule 60 min. midday for lunch and a walk. 3. Buy a wearable tracker (Apple Watch, Fitbit, Garmin, etc.).

I will track my success on my wearable.

My team will get a weekly report of my steps.

When I hit my weekly goal, we will hold a dance party. If the whole team participates, whoever gets the most steps picks the song!

LEADING OTHERS THROUGH UNCERTAINTY

When we've managed our fears and responded to adversity with resilience, we earn the right to lead others through the uncertainty. This is really at the core of leadership: the ability to guide others effectively when there isn't a clean, clear path forward. A leader's influence in these situations is huge and will often determine whether the team rallies or folds.

At Applied Leadership Partners, we believe that *leadership is a relational process of influence that yields results*. Those results aren't necessarily good or bad—that depends on the nature of the influence! Panic is contagious, but so is calm. A phrase that we used a ton in the Special Operations community was "Cool breeds cool." To effectively lead others through uncertainty, we must learn to generate a sense of calm that spreads to others.

Generating a sense of calm creates normalcy amid uncertainty. Normalcy abates our fears. In the SOF world, we consistently ran headlong into scary situations. Moving from a covered position into a building where you know an enemy is waiting is wholly unnatural, but we did it because we learned to do it calmly, and that was normal. Launching a new marketing campaign when the old one is working is scary. Bringing a new product to market is scary. Hiring a new leader is scary. Launching into new geographies is scary. All of this is scary because we move from our safe, covered position into the unknown. While we manage our fears accordingly, we must lead others to manage theirs or else face a common negative outcome: finding ourselves alone once we hit the goal. Let's not make that mistake. We need everyone to make it through with us. Here are six practical ways we can lead others through uncertainty:

1. Settle In and Temper Your Expectations: *Uncertain* means just that. We just aren't sure. Consider the unknown distance march and stop trying to guess when the circumstances will end. Setting our minds to mile 16 shatters our spirits come mile 17. It happens all the time. Leaders cast predictions or capitulate to the rumor mill. We say things like, "Maybe things will look different come September?" "Perhaps the market will turn next quarter, and we can hit our numbers?" "I think the supply chain will catch up next month, and then we can pound the pavement with our partners!"

Stop. We have to stop trying to predict the future. Let's lead now with who we have now. Let's sell now with the product we have now. Pivot to meet the customer now with what you can provide now. But let's stop casting false expectations about a future we cannot predict.

2. Tell the Truth: The truth is that the now is uncertain and, candidly, a bit frightening. There, we said it. There is always a way to appropriately acknowledge that things are tough without stoking the flames of fear. People are smart. If we're not being honest with them, even if it's to protect their feelings, they will know it. And they will likely fill in the blanks unfavorably. Also remember that while managing our fears and leading others through theirs, we will experience fatigue. No one can read our minds. If you're lost, say you're lost; if you're off target, say you're off target; and if you're hurting, say you're hurting, so your team can help solve the problem. Hiding a personal weakness will become a team liability. In that unknown distance march, if our teammates don't know that we are cramping and getting dizzy, they cannot help carry the load and nourish us.

We get to experience our humanity and limitations even as we lead others. Redistribution of load and delegation is vital in this endeavor. But we have to tell the truth about where the team is and where we are if we are going to get where we are going.

3. Encourage, Don't Complain: Leaders, the last thing we need is to hear one more person say "This sucks" amid adversity. We know! You can acknowledge the hardship, but don't belabor it! Be better. Call it what it is, make space for others to admit that it sucks, and then leave it behind.

Don't be afraid to host a five-minute bitch session. It's very straightforward and sounds like this: "Okay, everyone—we have five minutes to get it all out on the table. Say what you need to say, bitch, complain, moan, and gripe. And when these next five minutes are over, everyone will offer one thing they are thankful for, and we will talk about the next best step we can take."

4. Look for Signs of Unsettling: We must monitor our teammates and look for behavioral changes that indicate unsettling. This may sound like, "Hey, the team is asking me when you think this will end," or "Asking for a friend, but when do you think we can go back to normal?" Interpretation: "I've had it, and I want this to end. Now."

Signs of unsettling are teammate dependent. Look for the presence of the abnormal or the absence of the normal. A particularly social teammate may suddenly be more reserved. Or a typically stoic one may be especially chatty. These are signs of unsettling that cannot be ignored. Identify them and address them with candor and kindness.

5. Don't Go It Alone: Commit to coming alongside and encouraging one another when it's hard; you will get through this together. Engage and encourage. Acknowledge and affirm in those moments, but don't look the other way and hope it all goes away. It won't. People might—if they feel unseen—but problems won't.

We have an expression we use often: "Pass the tripod." In the military, machine gun teams must lug a heavy metal tripod around to mount the gun on. Passing off the tripod to share the load is common when moving long distances. In our business, we often ask one another to carry the tripod when we need it. It's how we ensure that we don't go it alone. It's how we tell the truth and ask for help.

Tell the truth. Ask for help. Who can you pass the tripod off to?

6. Never Leave a Fallen Comrade: We use tactical halts in the military. It's when we establish security for one another and allow time for necessary measures like changing socks, redistributing the tripod, sharing water, or checking our location and direction. A tactical halt to collect ourselves is a lot different from quitting. If you need to take a halt, take it.

Make time for a teammate to take a day off. Suggest they make their kid's soccer game. Push a self-imposed timeline back when appropriate. But don't leave your mates in the dust. That's not leadership. If Jeremiah had chosen to leave Brandon behind during the Best Ranger Competition, he could have shown that he was superior at the march that night. And he would have ended the competition for them both. Team competitions have no use for lone wolves.

———

If you're going it alone, you're not leading. Odds are you're excellent at your individual tasks and approach, but leadership requires more of us outside of ourselves. Leading teams to persevere through adversity requires us to keep the mission in perspective over the moment, manage our fears, and guide others through the uncertainty when change strikes. When we commit to this, we can engage the next factor of perseverance: acceptance

6

Acceptance: Clarity and Agency in Adversity

BLAYNE SMITH AND BRANDON YOUNG

Don't push the river, it flows by itself.
—*Ancient Chinese Proverb*

A s leaders, our first job is to see the world as it is, not as it was or how we wish it to be. We cannot effectively lead within a context we do not understand or refuse to accept. Denial is the enemy. It never helped make anything better. On the contrary, it is only when we accept our circumstances for what they are that we have any chance to find our way through them.

When we think about acceptance, we must understand that what we're actually striving for is clarity and agency. Once we can clearly see our situation and acknowledge that we have the power to influence it, we'll be in a position to move forward in a positive way. This is a critical concept to keep in mind. Too often, we confuse acceptance with throwing our hands up and turning over control. That's not it at all. Acceptance has nothing to do with quitting or just letting life happen to us; in fact, it's the opposite. At its core, acceptance is about responsibility. It's taking ownership of our life, with all its good and bad, and remembering that we get the final say on how things will go. We must stare our challenges right in the face and know we are the person to tackle them.

Clarity requires us to open our eyes and take a good look around. Through years of interactions, we've found that when a leader is unclear about what they or their team are up against, it is not because they can't see it but because they don't want to see it. Here's a simple example that we're sure you're familiar with: a kid falls and skins their knee, they're hurt, they start to cry, and then Mom or Dad (we'll admit our guilt up front) says something like, "You're okay, you're fine." Is that true? Is the kid really okay? No. And telling them that they're fine doesn't magically make it so. Their knee is bleeding, and they're in pain. In this example, the parent wants their kid to be okay. They want them to stop crying. They wish that the kid hadn't fallen down. But that is not the reality of the situation. The truth is that they've got an injured kid on their hands, and the child needs them to accept the fact that it's not going to be okay until they help.

This same dynamic plays out all the time in our professional lives. This might look like turning a blind eye to the bad behavior of a high performer. It could be glossing over a defect in a product that is already behind schedule. Whenever we avoid looking too closely because we're afraid of what we might find, we're missing an opportunity for clarity, and we'll almost always pay for it in the end.

Many things cause leaders to struggle to accept reality when life gets hard, but pressure is the biggest. Often we are under high pressure to perform and produce. Whether we are pushing for growth, efficiency, or excellence, many of us feel that we're constantly running along the razor's edge. The pressure may come from external sources like investors or the board of directors, or from internal ones like perfectionism or fear of failure. In almost all of these scenarios, the pressure is rooted in a belief that there is simply no margin for error. That may be the case in some instances—though it's often just perceived—but either way, we need to remember that ignoring one error will only lead to more numerous and more costly mistakes.

If we are unwilling to look at problems and accept them for what they are, we cannot effectively address them. This becomes especially true when our teammates stop bringing them to us, which will happen if we're not open to hearing bad news. We must be aware of how our posture influences the people around us. As leaders, we've got to remember that quiet is not to be confused with peace. Just because the team's issues stop showing up at our door does not mean that the problems no longer exist. In the same way our kid with the scraped knee will eventually stop turning to Mom and Dad for help if we tell the kid they're okay, our teammates will stop coming to us for support when things go wrong.

Once our team cuts us out of the loop, we totally lose sight of the on-the-ground truth and have no shot of solving problems because we won't see them until it's too late. If we want our teams to feel comfortable bringing us difficult news, then we shouldn't sit back and wait for these issues to land on our desks. We should proactively seek them out, setting a clear expectation that if something is wrong, we need to know about it. By doing this, we create environments that welcome challenges, not because we want things to be difficult, but because we want to see things clearly. One way to encourage a climate of candor about challenges is to reinvent the "open-door policy." Blayne shares his experience next.

———

I vividly remember sitting in our operations center in Kandahar, Afghanistan, and feeling the tension in the room. Our team was in the planning phase of a large operation to raid a Taliban-held village in the Arghandab River Valley. At that point, the intelligence on the target was inconclusive, the mission's objective was somewhat vague, and the team's motivation to plan and prepare was low. It was clear to me that the guys had some real concerns but were holding them back. It was uncomfortable because the task force headquarters was pushing this operation. I felt the pressure to make it happen, and I didn't want to disappoint them. On the other hand, I knew that something didn't feel quite right, and I certainly didn't want to compromise my team. So we sat around looking at each other, half-heartedly going through the motions.

I finally had to relieve the tension and say something.

"Fellas, I know that this op still has a lot of question marks, and I get the sense that at least some of you have some concerns about what we're doing. I need you to talk to me. This work is too dangerous, and we care about each other too much to launch a mission we don't feel good about. We're brothers here. You don't have the *right* to bring me your concerns about our operations; you have an *obligation* to bring me your concerns. That is what we owe each other."

———

Though this is something that we started during our time in the Special Operations world, it has continued to work wonders for our teams in the many years since: an "open-dialogue policy." Here is how it works. While a traditional open-door policy implies that a teammate *can* come to you with a concern, an open-dialogue policy requires that a teammate *must* share their worries or misgivings with the leader. This totally shifts the dynamic from one where our people are allowed to bring us problems to one where they are expected to, and this makes all the difference.

If we've got to find our way out of a dark valley, it is much better to know precisely where we are on the map and what the surrounding terrain looks like. If we delude ourselves into thinking that the high ground is just up ahead, it might feel nice at the moment, but it won't help us plot the best route and prepare appropriately for the journey ahead.

STOCKDALE PARADOX AND THE DUALITY OF HOPEFUL PRAGMATISM

When we hit a low point, it is easy to feel frustrated, disheartened, and uncertain about the future. And in these moments, we'd do well to take some advice from Admiral James Stockdale. Shot down over Vietnam in 1965, Stockdale spent eight years in the infamous Hanoi Hilton, where he was repeatedly isolated, tortured, and starved. It is hard to imagine how anybody could survive that kind of suffering, much less emerge to thrive. But he did, and his explanation of how was relatively simple.

The Stockdale Paradox, popularized by famous business author Jim Collins as a characteristic of great businesses, is essentially a combination of realism and resolve. You might call it hopeful pragmatism—the ability to face the brutal facts of our current reality while maintaining an unshakeable belief that we will prevail in the end. We can never lose hope, and we can never lose touch.

In trying times, pessimism is not the answer. It never is. But neither is pure optimism. In Stockdale's own words, "Oh, it's easy. I can tell you who didn't make it out. It was the optimists. They were the ones who always said, 'We're going to be out by Christmas.' Christmas would come, and it would go. And there would be another Christmas. And they died of a broken heart."[7]

These losses of life are heartbreaking to recall. Stockdale teaches us we can't simply wish away adversity and convince ourselves that it'll be over next month, or after the holidays, or at any arbitrary point on the calendar. We have to face the challenges in front of us and fight, and we have to do so knowing that we'll figure it out and make it through. This isn't paradoxical at all. It's the way that tough people have been solving problems forever.

When things feel totally out of control, it is easy to feel like we have to fall into one of two camps—"We're screwed" or "We're fine"—but we don't. The proper approach is to acknowledge that we're not screwed *and* we're not fine. We are in the middle of a bad situation. It hurts. And we don't know when it will be over. But we will work our way out of it.

If a particularly low moment has you feeling beat down, go easy on yourself; we all have our low points. Just keep Stockdale in mind. Shrink the world down a bit. Identify what is within your control. Accept that times are hard, take it one day at a time, and keep moving forward.

STOICISM'S DICHOTOMY (TRICHOTOMY) OF CONTROL

Admiral Stockdale attributed his remarkable perseverance through those torturous years largely to his practice of Stoicism. In one of his essays, titled "The World of Epictetus," Stockdale describes how studying Stoic philosophy at Stanford played a vital role in his survival. Long before Stoicism had a resurgence, he was a diligent student of the Stoic school of thought, and he shared these teachings with his fellow prisoners. At the core of this philosophy is a critical precept known as the Dichotomy of Control.

The Dichotomy of Control is a simple framework that instructs us to understand what is within our control and what is not. The Stoics believed that, to focus on life's most important tasks, we must be keenly aware of where our effort can actually make a difference. This is a vital step in the process because most of us greatly overestimate the degree to which we control our circumstances. As a result, we tend to waste a lot of energy fretting about and futilely opposing stuff that we cannot change.

Stoic philosophy constantly reminds us that we have no sway over the weather, the family we're born into, or the opinions of others. And rather than bemoaning this realization that so much is out of our hands, our goal is to simply accept the factors that fall outside of our control. While at first this approach may seem like we're giving up or ceding control of our life to the whims of the universe, that is not at all the intent. On the contrary, by letting go of what we cannot control—almost everything—we can focus all of our energy on the small number of things over which we have total dominion.

Accepting that so much of the world falls outside our purview frees us up to exert maximum effort on what is within our control, most of which is internal. We have sole discretion over where we place our attention, what we consume, and how much effort we put in. Of course, all of this takes discipline and practice, but we all can make these choices for ourselves. And by limiting (or ideally, eliminating) the time and energy we waste on things that we cannot affect, we regain the strength to prioritize the areas we can. Life and leadership are hard enough. Let's not make them harder by draining our batteries on stuff we can't do anything about.

Using the Dichotomy of Control is a helpful way to assess our situation and direct our focus to where it offers the best return. At first, the process can feel a bit black and white, but then, as we realize how complex many areas of life are, we have trouble sorting them into clear "zero control" or "total control" categories. There are some elements of our lives over which we lack total control but still have some influence. For example, we don't have ultimate control over how our children behave, but the way we parent will certainly have some influence. Similarly, our boss may have the final say-so on a business decision, but we may be able to nudge her in a particular direction. So, what do we do about these situations that seem to fall within some gray area—the circumstances where we can influence, but not dictate?

In his book *A Guide to the Good Life*, William Irvine offers us some assistance. He states that Stoicism's core tenet should be reframed as a "Trichotomy of Control" and suggests that we actually should consider three categories when deciding where to place our effort. Our two original buckets remain in play—some things will always fall completely outside of or within our control. However, Irvine submits that we need to add a third bucket for things that we cannot control but can still influence. This third category is a bit trickier to manage, but it is vital for keeping us engaged in the right kind of stuff. When we look closely at any situation, we're likely to identify many factors that we can influence. Sorting out which ones are worth our time can make all the difference.[8]

A method that we find helpful is to screen this category using a 2 × 2 matrix. Along the Y-axis, we consider the degree to which we have influence, ranging from very little to a great deal. Along the X-axis, we consider the degree of impact that this factor holds, ranging from low impact to high impact.

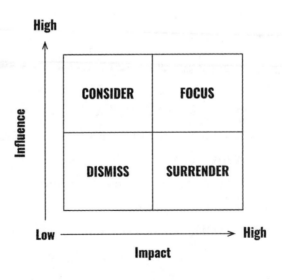

For variables of little impact, and over which we have little influence, we clearly do not want to spend a single second worrying. These things don't really matter, and we can't do much about them anyway, so we should *dismiss* them.

For those of little impact but that we have a high ability to influence, we may want to *consider* them briefly, but we won't want to give them too much effort. While we may be able to exert some influence, the juice is likely not worth the squeeze.

We are often tempted to spend disproportionate amounts of energy on variables that can make a significant difference in our lives but over which we have little or no influence. While we'd love to affect them, we probably cannot, and therefore we're simply raging against the river; it's best to *surrender*. These factors can be hard to accept because they feel unfair, unjust, or just plain wrong. But if we waste too much time hoping to change what we cannot, we leave ourselves with too little gas in the tank to tackle the fourth and most important (though often smallest) set of factors.

The top-right quadrant of our matrix is where we want to focus most of our attention. These factors can significantly affect our situation, and we have a high degree of influence over them. A simple example of these would be our diets. The type and quantity of food we eat has a massive impact on our health and the overall quality of our life. Diet is clearly an area that deserves our *focus*—our attention and effort. Yet, for most of us, this is not an area of life where we feel we have absolute control. Depending on where we live, our budget, our family, our schedule, and our culture, we won't have access to every type of food all the time. But still, if you're reading this book, you can almost certainly demonstrate a great deal of agency over your food choices. It may not always be easy, which is why so many of us struggle with it, but it is an essential part of our lives that can very significantly affect us.

The discipline to focus our energy on what we can control, or significantly influence, is a major step in developing our ability to persevere. We will find ourselves in positions that we do not like. We will come up against obstacles that feel completely unfair, even unjust. We must remember that while our position matters, our disposition ultimately matters more.

SURRENDER

If there is a single word that Special Operators are most allergic to, it is probably *surrender.* Unless it is immediately preceded by *never,* it will not pass the lips of a Green Beret, Navy SEAL, Marine Raider, or anybody else operating at the tip of the spear. Army Rangers stand in formation every morning and recite the Ranger Creed, which includes the line "Surrender is not a Ranger word" and concludes with "Readily will I display the intestinal fortitude required to fight on to the Ranger objective and complete the mission though I be the lone survivor."

The Special Operations community is trained to be unflinching and unwavering. These characteristics not only prepare operators to survive in combat but also day-to-day life in an elite unit. We are talking about a culture that demands excellence, is fiercely competitive, and allows no room for weakness. And the cardinal sin, the worst thing you can do, is quit, which is completely synonymous with surrender. Given the nature of the job, this makes sense. But if we look a little closer at surrender, we can find something truly powerful.

Surrender is such an interesting concept in modern culture because it is either taken in the military context and viewed as defeat or is conflated with apathy. But surrender, in its most profound sense, is not about giving up agency. In fact, it is just the opposite. Surrender is a commitment to take full responsibility for things within our control while releasing those that are not. It is having the maturity to let go of what has happened while remaining engaged in what is still happening.

If you have ever been surfing, you'll likely understand how this works. Surfing isn't so fun and addictive because we can paddle out into the ocean and dominate Mother Nature. We're not harnessing her power or imposing our will. All surfers know that if we fight against the ocean, the ocean will always win. To enjoy surfing, we must accept that on some days the waves will be great and on others they won't. We must accept that some waves are for us and others are not. And most importantly, we must respect the awesome power of the water and abide by its rhythms. Surfing is a crash course in learning that we are not in charge and cannot simply force things to happen. But surfing also teaches us that when we are willing to work with our circumstances and stay focused on our efforts, we can have absolutely amazing experiences.

There must be a reason why our most influential sources of wisdom implore us to surrender. If we look across the world's major spiritual and philosophical traditions, we see it everywhere. From the Buddhists to the Christians to the Stoics and the Toltecs, we are told that to live freely, we must first surrender. The Christian worldview even teaches that surrender leads to hope and new life, a light in the distance that Stockdale held in tension with the current situation.

We see adaptations of these teachings come to life in so many secular and practical ways. Those in recovery from drug or alcohol addictions have likely recited the Serenity Prayer many times. Step Three in the 12-step program is surrendering to the notion that there is a higher power—or at least a power greater than you! "Grant me the power to control what I can, accept what I cannot, and the wisdom to know the difference between the two."

If you've ever heard an interview with an NFL coach, you've noticed that they all talk about "the process." They know that even in the most competitive, cutthroat business on the planet, one cannot afford to get too wrapped up in the outcome and should instead focus on the process of preparing and executing. Make no mistake, these guys want to win. They need to win to keep their jobs! Yet they regularly encourage their teams to surrender the outcome.

And though you will never hear a Green Beret say the actual word *surrender*, you will hear them using some form of it all the time. The mindset of an operator going into a dangerous mission is one of preparedness and focus but also of peace because they have accepted the possibility that it could go badly, and they might not return. I've heard countless operators say something like, "I'm going to go through the door, and if it's my time, it's my time." The comments are sometimes lighthearted and sometimes dark, but they all acknowledge a lack of ultimate control. Your helicopter might crash, your parachute might not open, you could step on a mine, or face any number of other risks that you simply cannot mitigate down to zero. And the mission does not allow room for holding all of these contingencies in one's head. You've planned, prepared, and rehearsed all you can, and then it's time to let go.

Surrendering is especially important when things are going poorly—which is when we most want some control. When we're in a hole and badly want to change our situation, we don't want to be patient or "trust the process." We don't want to try something that might not work. But in these moments, our perseverance is essential, and we must accept that the road back may be long and difficult. These are the times when we have to have some faith and follow Teddy Roosevelt's advice to "do what you can, with what you've got, where you are."

EMBRACING THE SUCK

On the surface, there is nothing enjoyable about adversity. Yet, we all understand that there is often some longer-term benefit to our suffering. Mom, Dad, and coaches have all told us that our setbacks and hardships would help us build character. Millions of internet memes have reminded us that what doesn't kill us makes us stronger. We get it.

The problem, of course, is that none of this is much consolation when we are neck-deep in a round of layoffs, a serious injury, or a divorce. Our future selves may be better off for this, but right now, it really sucks. So what do we do about that? Counterintuitively, this is where we need to take our acceptance to a new level . . . to go from accepting our crappy situation to embracing it.

Special Forces selection and training are clearly intended to suck. It has a few cool aspects as you get closer to the end of the pipeline, but mostly it just sucks. Everything is done the hard way. It's not just that they take away all of your comforts; it's that they actively and constantly impose discomfort. The number of creative ways the instructors can make you cold, wet, sandy, disoriented, frustrated, or otherwise miserable is astounding. Day after day, week after week, month after month, it just continues to suck with no sign of letting up. And yet, young people not only volunteer for this torture, but they stick with it through all of the sweat and blisters and blood.

Blayne was one of those young people who eagerly took the punishment and made it through. He shares his insights next.

––––––

In the years since passing SFAS, dozens of people have asked me how I managed to hang in there when it got tough. And every time I am asked, I quickly inform them that they are asking the wrong question. Earning a Green Beret had very little to do with what I did. It had everything to do with why I did it.

I remember watching the Green Berets going into Afghanistan in the weeks after 9/11 and wishing so badly that I could be there with them . . . and not in the motor pool at Ft. Hood. As a Second Lieutenant, I pestered the Special Forces recruiters about submitting my packet. They were nice but basically said, "Slow down, Skippy, you've still got some work to do." They were right.

A couple of years later, I was a Scout Platoon Leader in Baghdad and had the privilege of working with some studs from the 5th Special Forces Group. At that point, the deal was sealed. If I was ever going back to war, I wanted to do it with these guys.

A few weeks after returning from Iraq, I went to SF Assessment and Selection. While there, I felt something in me shift. At one point, my burning competitive desire to "pass the test" gave way to something bigger. I no longer wanted to get selected for the Qualification Course—I needed to be a Green Beret.

One early morning, while we were waiting for the chow hall to open up—tired, sore, and dreading another day's worth of abuse—we were told to *"Make way!"* by an instructor. We all moved over so that a group of truly haggard-looking students could go to the front of the line. They were recently "liberated" SERE (Survival, Evasion, Resistance, Escape) school grads, and I remember thinking, *Damn, those dudes look wrecked.* Then I thought, *Shit, I'm wrecked! And if I think they're in rough shape, that course must be brutal.*

It was at that moment I realized that the completion of every training evolution is just a new starting line. I realized that difficult courses weren't about accomplishment, but preparation. In the years since, I've told every aspiring Green Beret that the key to passing Selection is simple: understand the work of an SF soldier, and if you need to do that work, you'll be fine. If you're looking to prove something to yourself or others or just love a good challenge, you're probably wasting your time. Because the long road to getting on an SF team is going to absolutely suck. It's going to suck for everybody, and one's success is not dependent on how much they reduce or avoid the suck but on the extent to which they embrace it.

———

It turns out that what truly matters when it comes to acceptance is our relationship to adversity. We can reframe our hardship in a way that doesn't make it suck less but instead makes it suck for a good reason. And when our suffering comes with significance, our ability to persevere is almost unlimited.

The vague promises of building character didn't make piano lessons or yard work feel any better as a kid because we were not at all invested in the outcome. We didn't understand what character meant or how it would help us get what we wanted out of life. We were just doing something unpleasant because we were told to, and it sucked.

But as we grew older and started to develop more deeply held goals and beliefs, we engaged in plenty of tasks that were much more difficult and unpleasant than yard work, and in many cases, we even may have enjoyed them. That's because we cared. When we are pursuing something that we care about, we are much more likely to gut it out during the hard times and see it through. When we have conviction in our mission, we know that adversity is part of the journey, and we accept it as such. In a way, the strain and discomfort signal that we are progressing and moving closer to our target. And this is what we need to remember on the dark, cold nights—that what we are going through is tied to a purpose. When we can reorient ourselves on why we are here, we can do better than endure and wait for it to end. We can embrace the suck and choose to persevere.

7

Choice: 3 AM in the Patrol Base

BLAYNE SMITH AND BRANDON YOUNG

> Somewhere. Some place. Some time, you're going to
> have to plant your feet, make a stand, and kick some
> ass. And when that time comes, you do it.
> —*Pat Riley (words of wisdom from his father)*

Knowing what we need to do is not the same as doing what we need to do. A moment of clarity and acceptance is precious, but at some point, we have to lace up our boots and get back to work. Once we've accepted the reality of our situation, we have to decide what we will do about it, because perseverance isn't so much a skill as it is a choice.

In the midst of every crucible, there comes a time when we have to decide whether we are up for the challenge. If you're reading this book, we trust that you are. We trust that you are willing to do what the situation requires. We trust that you are ready to rise to the occasion. Life is calling you toward your next breakthrough, to move through the adversity and become the leader you are capable of being. And we are right here with you along the way. So, let's consider how we choose to persevere by understanding the implications of options, instincts, and actions.

OBSESSING OVER OPTIONALITY

We tend to obsess about having options. Do we really need 26 kinds of orange juice to choose from at the grocery store? Doubtful. But in a world where we are all continually encouraged to refine our preferences, you can imagine how it happened. We no longer want much of what we use or consume to be merely sufficient; we want it to be just right. We are conditioned to believe that there is a perfect or individualized solution to our problems. In times of struggle, this belief holds us back.

Perhaps the only thing we love more than having options is keeping our options open. We tend to be far less committed than ever to our plans, jobs, and relationships. If you read a book about investing, you'll likely find a passage extolling the value of optionality, right next to a dizzying list of all the mutual funds available in your 401(k). This kind of diversification might be wise when constructing an investment portfolio, but in the rest of life, achieving optionality doesn't lead to success in and of itself. Having some flexibility and a menu of appealing options is certainly nice, but merely having options has no inherent value. None. All the value resides within the option itself—and none of that value is realized until we actually choose an option.

We can appreciate that this relatively new freedom and flexibility can be a wonderful thing for many people. But we also must recognize that for most of us, endless options have created an intense fear of missing out, or FOMO. And FOMO has become a potent driver of our behavior—especially as it relates to making choices. It is difficult to go all in on anything when we're constantly reminded that something "better" might soon come along. And while this is likely making us anxious and indecisive in our everyday lives, in moments of crisis it can paralyze us.

When life throws us a series of unexpected obstacles, taking some time to assess the situation and evaluate our options makes sense. A deep breath and a step back often help calm us down and allow us to refocus on what is truly important. However, we cannot stay in the waiting and assessing phase for too long. We must remember that while we don't want to make rash decisions, we also can't wait to make perfect decisions—those generally don't exist!

For leaders, finding a proper balance between rash and perfect can be incredibly difficult. On the one hand, we want to be quick and decisive. Our team may be in trouble or at a critical decision point, and we feel responsible for moving us forward. On the other hand, that feeling of responsibility can paralyze us with fear of making a wrong decision, forcing us to carefully consider all the possible options in the hope of finding a solution that will definitely work.

Consider the options restaurant owners faced throughout COVID-19. Typically, restaurants feed their patrons, patrons pay for their meals, staff get paid, and everyone wins. This worked fine until we were no longer allowed to enter restaurants, patrons no longer got their food, and workers ceased getting paid. Restaurant owners faced two basic options: pivot to takeout and delivery or shut down and wait. In retrospect, those who pivoted quickly tended to fare much better. They were able to keep feeding their customers and often found ways to keep staff on the payroll. Those who chose to shut down and contain costs, hoping to ride it out, struggled because reopening took much longer than most of us anticipated. But we couldn't have known that at the time. Besides, had the pandemic played out differently, those who decided to shut down completely might have looked very smart. But in reality, every restaurant had to make difficult, even existential choices in a highly uncertain environment. Many got it right from the get-go, and others found creative ways to stay in business after initially stumbling. As we navigated this unprecedented situation, all of us faced these kinds of choices in our own ways.

We continue to make hard choices every day we run our businesses. We are constantly confronted with the balance between executing the mission and caring for our people. This is why the US Army has a constant underlying axiom, "Mission first, people always," because choices emerge, invariably putting the two options in tension or friction as circumstances dictate. For instance, we need to initiate production, yet our engineers aren't pleased with the final design. We wish to keep our staff at full-time hours, yet we've taken a 20% reduction in revenue. Sales teams have closed the contracts, yet operations are understaffed to perform the services. Every day, we make choices and live with the associated trade-offs.

Success in life and leadership is not about having choices but about making them. No doubt you've heard countless stories of people telling you that they got accepted to a prestigious program, were offered a really impressive role, or had a chance to do this or that . . . but ultimately decided not to take it. Be honest. What do you feel in those moments? Are you super impressed that this person was able to generate an opportunity? Maybe, but probably not. We all can respect that earning an opportunity takes a certain amount of talent and hard work. But we also understand that we don't get credit for *being able to do something*. We get credit for *actually doing it*.

Being selected for Doctors Without Borders is cool, but giving up a comfortable life and a hefty salary to spend five years treating underserved patients in Africa is worthy of genuine admiration. Getting a bunch of big-time job offers is nice, but committing to a company and working hard to make it great is where we truly make a difference. Going on a bunch of dates is fun, but choosing a partner to love and share a life with is actually wonderful because you've done the work.

This is true in all things big and small. The value we bring as leaders has little to do with the options we can generate and everything to do with our ability to choose an option, apply committed effort, and make the very best of it. This is especially the case during times of trouble and turmoil. Taking action not only generates energy but also provides feedback. And that feedback can inform each subsequent step. So, let's remember that while making a choice may feel like limiting our options, it is likely opening up an entirely new set of possibilities.

DEVELOPING TRUSTWORTHY INSTINCTS

We've taken some time to discuss how we might overvalue options and undervalue the need to decide and move forward, but we haven't talked about how we make these choices. And though we agree strongly with General George S. Patton's belief that "a good plan, violently executed now, is better than a great plan next week," we also recognize that not all plans are good. That being the case, we need some way to evaluate our potential paths and determine which gives us our best chance to succeed.

Sadly, we can't produce a perfect algorithm that will make these decisions for us. But that's okay, because we can do better than that. If we are willing to engage our options with subtlety and nuance and all of the messiness that comes with being human, we can ultimately develop the judgment and instincts to make sound decisions with incomplete or imperfect information. We can ultimately develop trustworthy instincts.

Trustworthy instincts are where the gut and the head collide. Tested over time and refined through experience, they allow us to make sound, timely decisions in stressful situations—a superpower in today's world. Part of what makes humans so special is that we have both instincts and intellect. Like other animals, we are born with a set of innate abilities. There are things that we just know how to do (or know not to do) without ever being taught. Our instincts are powerful and play a critical role in moving through the world. They allow us to feel when something is right, a bit off, or dangerous. But they only take us so far. In fact, some of our natural instincts, the ones that kept our ancestors alive (gorging ourselves on calorie-dense foods, viewing new people as threats), can be counterproductive in modern times. Our environment has changed significantly over the past few thousand years, but our biology hasn't kept up. Fortunately, we also have the ability to reason with our intellect. We can document, share knowledge, and analyze the world around us. Humans are learning, meaning-making creatures who love to figure things out. We've got a lot going for us.

The challenge, of course, is how to blend all these remarkable abilities properly. How do we operate in this modern world without missing the facts or muting our instincts? We've got more stimuli, more data, and more distractions than ever in human history—and we still need to make sound decisions in life, love, and business. The variables are often complex and the stakes are high. So what do we do? How can we hone our instincts to make them truly trustworthy?

Part of the problem is that we tend to look at important decisions through two different and often opposing lenses. We are increasingly encouraged to be data driven—to avoid our unconscious biases and make decisions more analytically—yet we have a growing cadre of folks telling us to "go with your gut and follow your heart!" Either lens held separately is bad advice. No wonder we're confused!

To be truly effective as whole people, we have to integrate our faculties into a single lens. We must understand the quantifiable nature of decision-making in the context of our feelings, culture, and values. We can't (and won't) offer you a protocol or flowchart on how to make better decisions. And we certainly can't teach you to have perfect "Spidey Senses." We can, however, offer you a process to start developing trustworthy instincts—a framework to help you start merging the head and gut, all to help you make better choices.

As with everything we discuss, this is easier said than done. But we think you'll be well on your way if you follow these seven steps:

1. Orient: Before deciding, ask yourself some fundamental questions about the situation:

- What is it that you're trying to do?
- Where are you at right now?
- Where are you trying to go?
- How did you get here?

You can also explore some basic questions about yourself:

- What really matters to you?
- Who do you want to be?
- How do you want to show up in the world?

Understanding where you're at and who you are is a critical starting point from which to make crucial decisions. At first, it may take a little while—hours, maybe days—to answer some of these questions. But over time, the answers will come much more quickly, perhaps even subconsciously.

2. Acknowledge: When your intuition is talking to you, listen. Your "gut" combines physiological, intellectual, emotional, and spiritual factors that are shaped throughout your life. You may not fully understand where it comes from, but you know it's there—so don't ignore it! If your gut is talking to you, there is a reason. And while you shouldn't necessarily take your gut's advice at face value, consider what it offers. This brings you to the next step.

3. Process: Do you understand what your gut is trying to tell you? Have you been here before? Process what you feel in the way most suited to you. Write in a journal, go for a run, meditate, pray, breathe, doodle, whatever it takes. Do whatever helps you emerge with a better understanding of what you are feeling. Suspend judgment by taking words like *good* or *bad* out of the exercise. Some of your most significant breakthroughs may occur during these moments, so don't shut anything down before giving it some thought. Once you've taken the time and made the space for ideas to bubble up, shake out and organize your thoughts. One good way to do this is to write down each option you've generated in a sentence or two. Then, speak them all out loud and see how they feel. Sometimes, saying something out loud will make a given option seem ridiculous or obvious!

4. Compare: Does this gut feeling align or conflict with your initial orientation? Space out your reaction and your response. *Reacting* often stems from pure emotion—typically expressing base emotions like fear. On the other hand, *responding* is making the best decision possible with all available factors and feelings considered at the time. At this point, articulate your feelings or what your gut is driving you to do, and examine that against your stated goals and desired outcomes. Are your instincts pointing you in a direction consistent with who you are and who you're trying to become? Does the direction seem realistic and feasible, given the true nature of your situation and the factors at play? Or are there areas where your gut seems misaligned with what your analysis is telling you?

In this step, you want to square as much of this as possible before deciding. If some numbers or data seem counter to your instincts, pause and look more closely or seek an additional perspective. Likewise, if cultural norms point you in a direction that doesn't feel right, consider interrogating the status quo to determine the history and incentives that created it. In any case of perceived head–gut conflict, something is likely being over- or underappreciated—and you do yourself a service by going a level deeper to understand what's going on. In some instances, you may need to pay more attention to the spreadsheet, so to speak; in others, we may need to crumple it up and throw it away.

5. Decide: Make your call and move forward without delay. Execute with your full effort and enthusiasm—this part is essential. When you make a difficult decision or feel like you are in a 51%–49% situation, it's tempting to hedge or half-step your actions. You might think that if you're not completely sure of your decision, you shouldn't completely commit to executing it. But that's not a good approach.

Think about it like this. Let's say that you decide what to do and execute half-heartedly, and it goes poorly. At this point, what do you actually know? What have you learned? Not much! You don't know whether it was a poor decision or a good decision poorly executed. Even worse, you've spent valuable time and energy and are no better off than when you started—worse off, in fact.

Now, consider doing it differently. What if you make the call, then execute to the absolute best of your ability? In this scenario, there are only two possible outcomes, both positive. One outcome is success, which is obviously great, and the odds of getting this result only increase when you give it your full effort. The other is what we'd call a "well-informed failure," which isn't ideal, but still can be useful because now you've learned some-thing. You can proceed to something better, confident that this route was no good.

6. Reflect: Once you've decided and acted, you can assess how your choices are playing out. To reflect effectively, consider the results of a decision and the conditions within which you made it. It is normal but totally unfair to judge the decisions you or others make using the information and context we have today. If you knew then what you know now, you could have chosen differently, but that doesn't help you truly understand how and why you made a decision or if it was a good one. In your quest to develop trustworthy instincts, you'll need to discern whether your decision-making approach is serving you well. You can only do that if you are honest about what happened. To do this, ask some critical questions:

- What critical factors did you weigh when deciding?
- Which turned out to be more or less important than you thought?
- Did you make this decision primarily from your head or your gut?
- Was there any information that you should have consid-ered more closely?
- Was there a sense or feeling that you ignored?
- Did factors outside your control affect the outcome?

When asking and answering these questions, remember that making a good or even the "right" choice only partly influences the result. As mentioned, you can make the right call but still execute poorly. You can also make the right call but have your plans ruined by unforeseen obstacles. You can even make a poor decision, get lucky, and have things work out just fine. If you want to be confident and self-reliant in difficult situations, you'll need the discernment and intellectual honesty to reflect on the results of your decisions and develop your instincts over time. You cannot lose all self-confidence when one decision goes badly, nor can you have one work out well and start thinking that your instincts are infallible.

7. Refine: The beautiful thing about honest reflection is that it will help you learn and improve. If you can understand what happened, the decision that preceded it, and the process that drove the decision, you'll have everything you need to refine your instincts. You'll win some and you'll lose some, but you'll learn from them all. The key is to put that learning to good use, which requires a willingness to refine the way you approach tough decisions. Maybe you need to be better about seeking input, take the data more seriously, or listen more closely to the small voice that seems to know you so well. In any case, take every opportunity to understand yourself better. So, be sure to do something with the feedback from every difficult choice, because if you're not getting better, you're probably getting worse.

None of us ever will be able to completely feel or reason our way through life's most important decisions. We'll need to leverage our heads *and* our guts. Doing that takes awareness, practice, and diligence. But over time, we'll get better and more confident, and we will develop trustworthy instincts that will carry us through the adversities we face today and those that lie on the horizon tomorrow.

ACTIONS OVER INTENTIONS

The last critical piece to understand about choice is the importance of taking action. Simply generating good options or making good decisions is insufficient because they do no good without taking action. And as we mentioned at the beginning of this chapter, the difference between knowing what to do and actually doing it is massive. When persevering through adversity, we must make some very tough calls. The action required may be painful, disappoint people, and make us unpopular . . . at least for a while. In these circumstances, committing to doing what must be done takes courage, the ability to see the big picture, and a willingness to delay gratification. These are the moments when we truly choose to persevere. As the great Stoic philosopher Epictetus once said, "You can't hope to progress in areas where you have taken no action."

Note that when life is beating us down, taking action can feel overwhelming. It may seem that the distance between where we are and where we need to go is just too great. Maybe we understand what we need to do but aren't sure how to muster the energy or support to actually do it. This feeling is totally understandable, but it must be overcome. And the best way to do that is to shrink the world down.

Plenty of advice on the internet suggests that we need to have a bold vision and take massive action to achieve it, but when we're deep in the valley, that can feel like an impossibly tall order. The best approach is often to actually make things more manageable by thinking small.

We don't need to have it all figured out to make a choice and move forward. All we must do is commit to doing whatever it's going to take, which we can do one step at a time. We don't want to get bogged down with mapping out the perfect path or addressing every possible contingency. Instead, we want to consider our best next step. What is the first thing we need to do to get going in the right direction? It is that simple. By deliberately shrinking the world down to a manageable scale, we can shift our thinking from *What am I going to do?* to *What will I do next?*

For example, let's say that our friend goes to the doctor and learns that their health is at risk, and they need to lose 40 pounds—a seemingly daunting task. How can a person who has clearly struggled to maintain a healthy weight manage to lose 40 pounds? Our friend would seem to require a complete lifestyle transformation. We can imagine what they might be thinking. *How will I say no to Mom's home cooking? Will I be hungry all the time? Can I afford to buy healthier foods? Do I need to get a gym membership?* It is too much to contend with all at once.

But what if there were one or two steps that our friend could easily implement to get started? What if the doctor told them to (1) swap out their soda for seltzer and (2) walk for 20 minutes daily? Sure, that might take some effort, but it's certainly doable. Does our friend know what the next two steps will be? No, but they don't need to know, because right now, they just need to get started—to take positive action.

The beautiful thing about action is that it begets more action. Objects in motion tend to stay in motion. Taking one step gives us the opportunity and the confidence to take another and then another. Over time, these small choices add up and eventually compound. One mile becomes two, then three, then fifty. To persevere through adversity, we only need to commit to one thing—whatever is next. Even if the next thing we need to do is intimidating or painful, we must remember that we are taking this journey one step at a time. We learned this lesson very well at the US Army's Ranger School, the Army's premier combat leadership development course.

Let's be clear: Ranger School sucks. The days never really stop, but the transition from one to the next is generally marked by cadre changeover about 30 minutes before sunrise, or what we call BMNT (before morning nautical twilight). This is the time of day when the stars go away and the sun creeps toward the sky. Coincidentally, this is also the coldest part of the day. Shivering, with little to no sleep, the Ranger students provide security, clean weapons, conduct personal hygiene, and eat chow (always last), all while the Patrol Leader receives another mission from HQ.

The troops are bleary but steely eyed by dawn, a Ranger practice that has been in place since 1755. An hour or two later, the patrol initiates movement before completing the plan and spends the rest of the day patrolling under grueling weight through the woods, mountains, or swamps. At some point, the unit conducts reconnaissance of an objective, attacks an enemy position, withdraws, and moves to a new patrol base—where everything is repeated. Day after day, night after night. It is relentless.

A lot of weird stuff happens during the dark and hopeless hours between midnight and sunrise in a patrol base filled with 40 exhausted, starving, sleep-deprived Ranger students. There are countless (and mostly true) stories of Rangers mistaking trees for vending machines, talking to shrubs, hallucinating an enemy in front of their position, and many other oddities you rarely see anywhere else. On any given night, at least half the class is in survival mode and mostly useless, which makes leadership especially difficult: sleep may be an option for an individual contributor, but not for the Patrol Leader. Each night, to receive a passing grade on their patrol, the leader must ensure that security is continuously maintained while all priorities of work are accomplished. And none of this will likely happen without some serious personal involvement from the leaders. This is particularly true during the dark, cold witching hour of the night: 3 AM.

Three AM in the patrol base is when you make your money as a leader. Stumbling through the camp amid the scattered, shivering bodies, you must focus on the tasks at hand to accomplish the mission. Leaders can't "mail it in" at this hour. At a time when most of the platoon is at their worst, leaders need to be at their best. The work required to accomplish the mission is not especially complex or profound. It just sucks. This is just as true in life and business. There will always be times when the right thing to do is obvious but totally unappealing, and this is when we earn our salt. *"3 AM in the patrol base" is when the last thing you want to do is the first thing you need to do.*

Our "3 AM tasks" can make or break us. In Ranger School, it's when we check the position of the machine guns to create the best security perimeter for the platoon. In our organizations, it might look like a weekly report, monthly client update, or project that we haven't gotten to. It is when we've worked a full day, done our job, maybe even gone the extra mile, and still have additional responsibilities that are wholly ours or delegated tasks that we must monitor for mission success.

Although at 3 AM we may be exhausted and our capacities degraded, we still have to check on the welfare of our people. We have to ensure that the perimeter is secure and the guns are clean, so we need to get up and move . . . because soon the sun will be up, and the patrol must be ready for the next mission. We have to dig deep in these moments. In Ranger School, the difference between getting a "GO" to graduate or earning a "NO-GO" and re-cycling is the willingness to choose the hard right over the easy wrong at 3 AM in the patrol base. In business, it might be the difference between your next professional breakthrough or another year of subpar performance.

You've put in the work—of that we have no doubt. We know you're tired and hungry and deserve a little reprieve. But this is when your people need you most. Checking the guns at 3 AM isn't glamorous and likely will go unappreciated—until it isn't done and the patrol gets overrun. Trust us when we say that your willingness to make a choice and follow through consistently and intentionally, compounded over time, will ultimately breed mission and team success.

If you can imagine a young, frightened, and freezing soldier choosing to take one good next step when they are starving and hallucinating, can you imagine making your next choice right now? Place your choices before you. Can you see them mapped out across the board? What is your gut telling you? What are your closest advisors and supporters telling you? What does the team need right now? Not what do we want—what do we *need*? What must you do, right now, to take one small step toward success? Put another way, what is the one thing you know you need to do but do not want to do? Wherever we are tempted to look away from is most likely where we need to look into.

Now is the time. This is when we choose to become the leader the situation calls for. It's 3 AM in the patrol base, leader. What needs to get done? Identify it and do it! Progress is within your grasp in the present; growth awaits in your future.

8

Growth: The Perseverance Payoff

BLAYNE SMITH AND BRANDON YOUNG

> One can choose to go back toward safety or forward
> toward growth. Growth must be chosen again and
> again; fear must be overcome again and again.
> —*Abraham Maslow*

The preceding four factors of perseverance—change, uncertainty, acceptance, and choice—occur during adversity, regardless of what you do. But not growth. Adversity brings about change. Change is fraught with uncertainty. You can accept this with or without doing anything about it, which is a choice. Choice gives us agency, but let's be clear—the agency to do what? We *can* choose to stay stuck in the suffering. We *can* endure and thereby survive but still fail to thrive. Those are choices, but not *the* choice of a leader who aims to persevere through adversity and forge a tighter, more effective team in the process. The choice to persevere is the stage gate to growth. *Where choice is the crucible of perseverance, growth is the outcome.*

Choosing to persevere is choosing to grow into the leader the situation calls for and the person that life invites us to be. When we grow, we become our creeds, our values, and our ethos in service to our mission and our people. When we grow, we stop talking about values and start becoming them. The growth we experience through perseverance generates wisdom, increases leadership capabilities, and provides the confidence to move boldly forward into greater challenges.

When we persevere through to the other side of adversity, we are not just someone who did something, but the kind of person who does things. The perseverance payoff is not the achievement (though you will achieve). It's becoming the type of leader who can persevere through adversity and win when it counts the most—a wiser, more effective, and more sustainable leader who guides teams through the complexity of our times.

WISDOM IN THE AGE OF INFORMATION

Being a human is hard, particularly in an information age that baits us into believing that all knowledge is a commodity of equal merit, regardless of context. But volume does not equal value. Knowledge on its own is, in fact, useless without the understanding and application that generates wisdom. The ancients knew this. And though the digital age continuously tries to convince us otherwise, we are not smarter than the ancients because we have more access to information. Not by a long shot.

Knowledge, understanding, and wisdom are each important yet uniquely different.

Knowledge is our collection of information, facts, skills, and data. Like colored marbles in a bag, knowledge can be collected and used—sometimes for little more than amusement and observation. You've all heard that "knowledge is power," but we think it is better described as potential energy.

Understanding is the awareness of where information comes from and how to apply it correctly. Understanding takes data collection and places discrete items within their proper contexts for their intended purposes. A tangerine is a spherical orange object, but you wouldn't play basketball with it. No, that requires a different spherical orange object. Both could be sorted into similar descriptions, but neither meets the same purpose—a basketball is for playing, a tangerine is for eating. Understanding that difference makes a big difference.

Wisdom is gained over time by applying our knowledge and understanding to the right situations, at the right time, in their proper context. Wisdom grows when we consider the impact of our actions on the people and world around us. We become wise not through acquiring pure knowledge or even understanding that knowledge, but by learning if, when, where, and how to apply it.

Consider it this way: if you aim to build a house, you must have all three components. First, you must count the costs and collect the boards, nails, and other materials (knowledge). Then, you must have the direction to assemble those materials in the form of a blueprint (understanding). Last, you must combine those materials with blueprints and construct the house. You must actually cut the boards, assemble the angles, drive the nails, and turn the screws. When you do, you will discover that no straight line exists outside of that blueprint. You've got to get your hands dirty and see where the pitfalls are, how frequently you must adjust to accomplish the intent of the blueprint, and what it looks like when completed. This is wisdom. Wise leaders have built houses. They know that no two are exactly the same and that none of them go up without plenty of setbacks. Wise leaders know every house requires more than just materials and blueprints.

Likewise, wisdom requires more than data and details. Wisdom requires context, courage, and moral reasoning. A 2019 task force of psychology researchers grasped this when they submitted a definition of wisdom to the social sciences. They "defined wisdom as morally grounded reasoning and problem-solving in situational domains that have the potential to affect other people."[9] This provides a solid definition of wisdom. Still, the great figures upon which Western society was built—Moses, Solomon, Plato, Aristotle, and Jesus—also knew wisdom in more intimate ways than merely conceptually.

Wisdom abides within the heart—the very center of volition and reason. Wisdom enables the discernment between good and bad, right and wrong, and positive and negative. The ancients saw wisdom as enabling one to live life to the fullest with a richness that would benefit the individual and the community. They understood wisdom's power so keenly that they spoke of it as a living force active in the world and within us. You may be familiar with the name of wisdom personified in the Greek—*Sophia* (Σοφία)—an agent who is predated by the far less elegant sounding yet equally unrivaled Hebrew *ḥā·ḵə·mōwṯ* (חָכְמוֹת), or Lady Wisdom. Wisdom was expressed in all of these ways, in addition to living wisely, which led to good business sense, high esteem, happiness, and so on. And they knew that wisdom does not come easy.

Whether ancient or modern, lived out or inherent, wisdom grows through time and experience. Wisdom grows when we consistently do the work. Wisdom sits at the apex because it is the outcome of applied knowledge and understanding. Wise leaders are rooted, unshakeable leaders who embrace new challenges, knowing that they lead to greater skill and capabilities. Our world needs more wisdom. We humans have tested the deluge of data upon our consciousness and seen that while information brings knowledge and, at times, understanding, it does not generate wisdom because information is neutral and impersonal. By contrast, wisdom is wholly animated and required for the complexities of real life.

The desire for wisdom is growing. In 2023, an analysis of 30 years of research publications showed that before the 1980s, only 10 papers with the keyword *wisdom* in the title were published in peer-reviewed journals per decade. That figure increased in the 1990s to 73, shot up to 375 in the 2000s, and nearly doubled to 720 papers from 2010 to 2023.[10] The rising interest in better understanding wisdom over the last three decades has matched the rise in access to information through the internet. "When Pew Research Center began systematically tracking Americans' internet usage in early 2000, about half of all adults were already online . . . [as of January 2024] . . . 95% of U.S. adults say they use the internet."[11] Access to information has become ubiquitous in modern life, but it hasn't necessarily increased understanding. And wisdom continues to elude. Researchers Mengxi Dong, Nic M. Weststrate, and Marc A. Fournier see the increase of wisdom as a critical need in our information age:

As the world becomes more complex and polarized, and the future of humanity more uncertain, it is increasingly clear that people need more than just knowledge, intelligence, or skill to manage the challenges and failings of modernity. People must navigate through a sea of information, misinformation, and disinformation; balance seemingly contradictory goals (e.g., protecting vulnerable people vs. sustaining the economy during a pandemic); and effectively collaborate to reach working agreements with people who hold divergent viewpoints and values.[13]

More simply stated, people need wisdom. Perseverance increases wisdom. As we have stated, a crisis puts a microscope on our existing problems far more than it tends to create them. Real adversity breaks the misconception that information is of greater value than understanding and wisdom. Persevering through adversity teaches us the differences among the three and forges the character that carries us to the other side.

Growth on the other side of perseverance brings about power in leaders that appears as a noticeable calm and humility. It is clear that they wholly own their wisdom, yet it has cost them something along the way. If wisdom is the outcome of why we grow, pride is the cost. Growth gives us what we need but rarely offers what we want.

WHAT WE NEED, NOT WHAT WE WANT

We are all confronted by our limitations when it's time to persevere. Growth occurs when we become aware of our blind spots, apply discipline and humility to address them, and prioritize our purpose over our pain in the process. Growth begins with awareness, and the role of other leaders in the process cannot be overstated. As leaders, we need other leaders to challenge and encourage us to be our better selves because we all have blind spots.

Blind spots are those aspects of our disposition, training, and experiences that lie hidden below our consciousness yet are plainly visible to our compatriots. *We all have them.* Blind spots cause disruptions within the team and must be addressed if we hope to grow. Having them is not the problem. Ignoring them, refusing to address them, and fighting others who make us aware of them is.

Blind spots are where we often get hit the hardest. The risk that we don't see coming is always the one that crushes us. And we will keep getting crushed if we remain too proud to accept correction. This is why being called an "individual" in the Army is an insult. Individuals rely only upon themselves; teammates rely on each other. Rangers have no use for individuals, so they are systematically sniffed out during assessment and selection. In Ranger School, every class cycle conducts something called Peer Evaluations—"Peers" for short. They present an opportunity to lift the curtain that the cadre cannot see behind and to offer insights into all the candidates' real behaviors— what they do when the instructors are not watching.

You learn a lot about character in the barracks, at chow distribution, weapons cleaning, or during other monotonous tasks. During Peers, you learn that someone is always watching. Every candidate gets feedback, but the peer-review process culminates in listing the bottom three members of the squad based on their patterns of poor performance or character. These are the guys that you wouldn't want to go to war with.

Being told that your peers wouldn't want to go to war with you is a hard pill to swallow; essentially, your comrades have just told you that you are not up to the standard, and that hurts. But sometimes it's the medicine you need most, especially if your ego is keeping you from your next big breakthrough. Pride keeps us shackled to our deficiencies, while humility allows us the freedom to grow. Pride is the enemy of growth. Humility is growth's ally.

Also, Peers aren't merely written reviews. Rangers are required to read their peer reports directly to their comrades. The feedback process is about competency, not compatibility, and the objective in high-performing teams is collegiality—not likability. Whether or not you like another Ranger (or colleague) is entirely irrelevant. When you're part of a team, performance and character are all that matter. Delivering Peers personally provides a growth opportunity for all involved.

During Peers, Rangers provide the observed issue to their comrade, discuss the details involved, and suggest how the other Ranger needs to improve. This ensures that Peer Reviews remain an opportunity for constructive criticism, not destructive gossip. Patterns of deficiencies emerge, and the bottom three candidates are counted by the total number of peers who identified the same blind spots.

After Peers, the young Rangers are offered the chance to course-correct and are dismissed if unwilling. Rangers' pride or humility are exposed glaringly at this moment. The humble change and grow into capable leaders. The prideful don't and find themselves elsewhere, typically with a story about how they got "screwed" in Ranger School.

Before addressing how we grow into our blind spots, we should address how to respond when they emerge. Perseverance will expose our blind spots. We don't have to have an intense peer-evaluation session to learn where we are lacking as leaders. When those blind spots are exposed, our egos can feel bruised. Yet we can fight against them or embrace them and transform. Here are six simple yet hard responses to handling blind spots that lead to maximum growth:

1. *The Window and the Mirror*: This model has been used across many leadership approaches and is a staple in the US Army Special Operations community. Simply stated, when someone receives criticism, there are two common responses—either they point the finger out at everyone (looking through the window), or they turn their attention back on themselves (the mirror). Always choose the mirror. Instead of firing away at everyone else, take aim at yourself. Look yourself in the mirror and ask, *What can I learn from this? How can I grow through this? Though I may not like what I've heard, what part of it may be true?* Looking in the mirror is the first act of agency in an otherwise off-balance situation.

2. *Asshole Math*: If you think one person is an asshole, they're probably an asshole. If you think five people are assholes, you're probably the asshole. The numbers won't lie on this. If your team has told you the problems they observed and your response is to dismiss them, then *you* are the problem. If you rationalize with *They just don't like me, they are jealous of me, they all conspired against me . . .* those are signs that it's

probably not them; it's you. Do the math. Talk to a trusted advisor and grow.

3. *Seek Responsibility and Take Responsibility for Your Actions*: This is drilled into every single Ranger from day one. Heeding constructive criticism is a chance to take responsibility for your actions and your faults—and to take ownership of your growth and your future.

4. *Put Down Your Shield and Pick Up Your Pencil*: It's natural, after being informed of one's blind spots, to perceive that you just got attacked and to feel the need to defend yourself. Don't. Instead of picking up your shield, pick up your pencil and take notes. Ask questions to understand better. Far too many people walk through life with blind spots because we have lost the art of sharing difficult feedback with each other. Try to receive feedback—even if it feels like criticism—as a gift.

5. *Stop Making Excuses*: We can excuse ourselves from growth our entire lives. If we're smart, we can try litigating every point of improvement that someone gives us. Both are foolish and counterproductive. Explaining away each and every criticism will only keep us stuck. We'd do better to step back and view the larger whole, accept feedback, and try to grow.

6. *Grow Up*: Don't pout like a child. Grow like a professional. All professionals subscribe to a set of qualifications, expectations, norms, and guidelines specific to their field. If we've been called out of line on any of those matters, then we need to fix ourselves. Period.

As it turns out, a prideful reaction to having our blind spots exposed is common. That's because no one—regardless of relationship, industry, or level of professional tenure—is immune to being human and feeling hurt. One of the gifts of adversity is that it forces us to confront our blind spots, typically because they feel like affronts. We cannot unsee them amid the struggle. Perhaps our messages keep missing the mark no matter how many times we try to communicate them, or our biases are on display no matter how much we know the sunk-cost fallacy can swamp us, or our decisions get made by proxy because we failed to act and the market acted for us.

Choosing to persevere forces us to deal with our blind spots, and dealing with them requires a series of courageous acts of follow-through. It takes guts to own our weaknesses. It takes discipline to do something about them.

DISCIPLINE DECODED

Discipline is the ability to consistently choose what we want *most* over what we want *right now*. Discipline is being who we say we are and doing what we say we are going to do. It's simple and it's hard, but it's not out of reach.

Contrary to popular belief, discipline is not a superpower. Yet many people still find the origin of discipline to be a mystery. They say, "I wish I had that kind of discipline, but I just don't." Discipline is not special or unique to those who exercise it. Rather, the secret about discipline is hiding in plain sight: you show up and do the work, even when it's hard and especially when you don't want to. Mystery solved.

Society has made discipline very hard on people, amid a culture that tells us to do what *feels* good over what *is* good. We suggest that discipline *is* good and that we must reclaim it from all the baggage it is saddled with if we aim to grow. There are good reasons why discipline is so prickly, so let's address them.

Though discipline is both an action and an outcome, talking about it gets sticky because we often focus on the former rather than the latter, and being disciplined leaves lasting impressions. The very root for discipline in Hebrew, *yasar* (יָסַר), or Greek, *paideia* (παιδεία), relates to sharp instruction (of a child or follower): training, chastening, admonishment, or correction. It's not hard to see why we tend to look away from discipline. I mean, who wants to be corrected, chastened, or admonished? No one does. But focusing on the process over the outcome in this sense makes it easy for us to shy away from some of the fruits of discipline, such as restraint, consistency, courtesy, respect, and follow-through.

Who wants the results of that process? Who wants discipline that yields consistency, restraint, diligence, and excellence? Everybody. Every leader. Every team. That being the truth, we must find a way to embrace discipline productively. The purpose of discipline has always been (and will always be) to grow desirable human practices and qualities, such as resilience and perseverance in the face of adversity.

Exercising discipline toward our values and mission offers us stability in ambiguity and a path toward growth when it's hard. Discipline to our values and mission offers us resilience in times of trouble. When a challenge is far too large to see an obvious way out of it, discipline invites us to shrink the world down into one little act of progress toward the goal. If we are going to exercise discipline and grow, we need to keep our mission in keen focus and our values in plain sight. We likewise must deploy discipline in moments when our blind spots confront us. When life serves us a heaping helping of tough feedback, addressing our revealed blind spots in service to those collective values and the team's mission is a great place to start.

We often find, however, that people aren't totally clear on their personal values. This is where communities like the military and religion help greatly—they've already sorted out their values. Nearly every team in this era has a set of collective values they prescribe. It's easy to see why integrity is one of Blayne's core values. After all, from ages 18 through 22, he passed by an Honor Code sign in front of Washington Hall at West Point that read "A cadet will not lie, cheat, or steal, or tolerate those who do." It's easy to discover why faith is one of Brandon's core values. After all, he holds a master of divinity degree and is rooted in verses such as "Trust in the Lord with all your heart and lean not on your own understanding" (Proverbs 3:5).

Having difficulty identifying our values is normal. We can't discipline our actions to our values if we don't know what values we're aiming for in the first place. The good news is we don't have to go through intense military training or a long graduate school program to sort this out. Still, whether or not your team has a collective set of values, identifying our *individual* core values is critical. Brené Brown's Dare to Lead List of Values[13] is a great place to start. Brown offers more than 40 commonly held values you can browse to see which ones resonate most. Then you have to do the harder work of narrowing that list down to only two or three that you identify with the most. We highly recommend it!

Regardless of whether we've contemplated what we believe our values to be, facing adversity will certainly help us to uncover what we *actually* value. We discover what we truly care about and what we are willing to fight for. This process can be a bit of a reckoning. We sometimes realize that our stated values don't completely overlap with our revealed values, and that's okay because this is how we grow. Once we are clear on our core values, we will find it easier to persevere, knowing why we are doing this in the first place!

THE POWER OF PURPOSE

Purpose propels us toward growth in service of our mission and our people. *Why do you do what you do?* Not just why your company does what it does, or how your team operates to achieve its goals, but why do *you* do what *you* do? This is the critical, personal question that we must answer in the crucible. When everything else is scraped away, and you have nothing left but your will and your choices, why will you fight on? Why *must* you persevere? Not why do you *want* to persevere; why do you *have* to persevere? Now is the time to answer these questions because we all must find our purpose to persevere when it gets unbearable. For whom? For what?

Simon Sinek has benefited all leaders with his seminal work, *Start with Why*. We applied the construct effectively while forming our business and often in the early Team RWB days. Sinek reminded us how the Wright Brothers started with why and inspired their team to take flight. How Steve Jobs and Steve Wozniak started with why and inspired the personal computer revolution that launched Apple's music, smartphone, and small electronics businesses. And how

Dr. Martin Luther King Jr. started with why and went on to amplify the civil rights movement that transformed America with four words: "I have a dream."[14]

These examples remind us how great leaders prioritize purpose and inspire teams to accomplish incredible feats. Each of these leaders had an internal purpose driving their obsession for advancement, then fought for it. Every great leader learns what they are willing to fight for in the fire. We can talk all we want about blind spots, discipline, and humility, but all of those are vehicles of growth that must be pointed in the direction of our purpose. Rangers and Green Berets know this better than just about anybody else.

Ranger and Green Beret candidates become wise in purpose amid assessment and selection because all other knowledge and understanding are dashed against the rocks in the process. Selection is designed to break you, to shatter your expectations and push you beyond your perceived limits, so all that remains is your purpose and the will to carry on. Blayne shared his experience of SFAS as a candidate earlier in the book. Brandon's experience is interesting because he has been on both sides of the assessment and selection process (candidate and cadre) and knows how the program is intentionally constructed to push candidates past their breaking point. He shares this peek behind the curtain of RASP to highlight the importance of purpose in the process of growth.

———

Cole Range lies in the backwoods of Ft. Moore (formerly Ft. Benning) at the edge of Jamestown and Yankee Roads, the intersection of dreams and reality, of hope and pain. Aside from the orange diamond sign, it is an otherwise indistinct plot of land with a 300 × 250-meter field nestled between two land navigation courses. It is a place where deep suffering occurs.

"Build a fire . . . a big one. As high as my head and as hot as the sun," I said coldly.

"Roger, Sergeant!" the Army private replied through chattering teeth.

He had just pulled his gear over to the cadre shed, escaping the rain and the pain of the class formation. He was the first to quit that night; we knew he wouldn't be the last. It was another sleeting winter night at Cole Range, where smarts, strength, and stamina are merely the price of admission. Much more is required of everyone to make it through.

The 200-man Ranger Assessment and Selection Program class struggled to stand at the position of attention while the wind and rain racked their bodies.

"It's going to be a long night," my partner said flatly.

At 6'2" and 240 pounds of muscle, Andy was fast, strong, smart, and terrifying. Our platoon sergeant, Ed, who helped raise me in the 2nd Ranger Battalion, looked on with approval. He is much smaller in stature than Andy and me, yet larger than life in presence.

Being a Ranger isn't for everyone. The saying goes, "Not for the Weak or Faint Hearted," but even if you are strong and resolute, Rangering still is not for everyone. It is a 24/7, zero-defect calling that requires everything of you. A Ranger's life is highlighted by sacrifice, pain, brutality, and excellence—and that's just the job. The lifestyle of a Ranger is one of character, determination, leadership, discipline, and a lifelong brotherhood. That's what America expects of its premier large-scale Special Operations raid force. The assessment and selection process is an uncompromising commitment to finding those who possess the skill and the will to live that life at the tip of the spear.

And if you're not able or willing to be that person, to live that creed every day, you are a threat to your fellow Rangers and the mission. Honestly, you're a threat to yourself because no one's a *sorta* Ranger in the 75th Ranger Regiment. It's a "100% and then some" proposition, and the RASP cadre's job is to ensure that message is clear.

We patiently wait as the fire gets going, close enough for the formation to see it but far enough to prevent them from feeling the heat.

"Now is the time that you get to decide if you really want to be a Ranger," I add.

Jaws tighten as the frigid formation strains to keep their feet grounded while at attention.

"This life is not for everyone. We know that many of you have doubts. If you're weighing those doubts, feel free to step to the fire."

Doubt is not inherently bad. Doubt can lead to curiosity and humility in life. But doubt can kill you and your mates in combat. Doubt untethered to purpose leads to a lack of commitment.

Everyone who stands in formation at Cole Range has doubts once the games begin. At one time or another, we all wondered why selection had to be so hard. I got my answer during Winter Strike 2003—starved, exhausted, and flea ridden. I understood at that moment why RASP had to be so hard. The challenge for a Ranger candidate is to identify their own purpose for being there and to hold on to that purpose tightly when the storm sweeps through them. And it will sweep through them. The storm sweeps through everyone.

This is where all of us can relate. All of us have faced storms in life—divorce, loss of employment, sickness, rejection, failure, and so on. We can all relate to being in a miserable situation, straining to get from where we are to where we want to be. I found my purpose while suffering as a young Ranger hopeful. I was just another American kid left behind by his father. I wanted to be somebody after always feeling like a nobody. I wanted to be a part of something after being left to feel that I was nothing. I stood in that very formation in 1998 and found what carried me through the selection. With every drop of rain that sent icicles down my back, every sprint to the woodline, every push-up, every ruck march, and every land navigation course, my resolve strengthened.

I needed to be an Airborne Ranger. I am an Airborne Ranger.

Though everyone's reason for suffering through RASP is personal, the fact that everyone who makes it has a reason is universal. And that's critical for persevering through adversity. Knowing your why is critical to experiencing growth amid the hardship.

By midnight, the group of men huddling by the fire is larger, while the formation of Ranger hopefuls is smaller. Hope can be crushed when you realize that the pain will not stop. And at Cole Range, the pain does not stop.

"Hit the woodline, men."

The beleaguered men sprint the quarter-mile field to the woods and back again, gaining reprieve from the cold, but not for long. Shortly, they are back in formation, getting battered by the sleet. The cold wrecks everyone. You learn that in the military. Cold is a powerful equalizer that eliminates partial motivation and false hopes.

"Again. Woodline. Hit it!" The ragged and gangling mob slogs across the open field to the silent woods that have witnessed thousands of broken dreams. That field will claim more dreams before dawn.

Back in formation, the men hold their ground and hold on for dear life. We barely look at them and speak casually to those gathered by the fire. "You guys look like you could use some rest," I say. "Open up that box truck and start pulling out sleeping bags."

Though the rain is relentless, the uniforms of the men beside the fire are dry. Their eyes stay fixed upon the flames, never daring to glance at the formation on the field.

No quarter is given at Cole Range; none is given in combat.

"Again!" Andy shouts.

Knees buckle. Tears fall. Men break.

And it lasts for hours.

"Hit the woodline!"

Bodies drop.

"Again!"

Men are trampled.

"Hit the woodline!"

Hopes are shattered.

Those who quit file by the truck to collect a meal and a sleeping bag. Those who remain in formation have none of these comforts, but they all have a common possession: purpose. Purpose underpins their commitment. Purpose transcends the cold, the discomfort, the frustration, the helplessness, and the hopelessness. Purpose is the great separator between those who want to be Rangers and those who *have* to be Rangers.

By dawn, the rain lets up as Ed, Andy, and I complete our responsibilities for the shift. We will go home and rest for the next 24 hours. The men in formation will stay, along with a fresh team of Ranger cadre. A ray of sunshine pokes a glimmer of hope through the clouds while more than 60 soldiers snooze peacefully by the fire, their bodies free from the nightmare on the field, their dreams of becoming Rangers dying with the embers of the fire.

In formation, the starved, the sleepy, and the battered shiver 50 feet from the fire and one day closer to becoming a Ranger. Never looking upon the fire for a moment, their eyes purposefully fixed upon their goal in the distance.

Rangering isn't for everyone.

What the Rangers know about weeding out the weak is that the only difference between the men in formation and the men at the fire is the willingness to suffer until your purpose is achieved. What the Rangers know about persevering through adversity is that purpose pulls you through when it's harder than you ever could have imagined. What the Rangers know about adversity is that everyone will face it eventually, and while adversity changes you forever, adversity never lasts forever.

———

We imagine it can be hard to understand why any young person would put themselves in the position to suffer through assessment and selection. We also trust that you can extract the point: you simply need to know why you *must* persevere. This brand of purpose keeps us in the fight, even if we aren't sure that we can make it through. It's a purpose that empowers us to find a way, to figure it out, and to become the person that the journey requires us to be.

Our sense of purpose is the power that pulls us through the suffering, and growth is the treasure hidden in the dark. Purpose drives us toward that growth, which only comes at the end of perseverance. When confronted with a choice between the harder road and the path of least resistance, we either opt to run *toward* our purpose or run *away from* our pain. If we lack a clear understanding of "For whom?" and "For what?" we are far less likely to keep moving toward the summit and far more likely to drift into the swamp.

As we stated, you may not understand it while persevering, and you may not immediately feel whole on the other end of it. It took Brandon years to feel like a whole part of his family after so much war, loss, and separation. It took Blayne years to feel whole after the loss of his teammates. And while none of those tragedies "had to happen for us to grow," as so many casual platitudes go, the fact is that they did happen. And we chose to grow amid those crucibles because growing was the only way to stay on the path. We rejected the myth that life was happening to us. When life was at its worst, we accepted the challenge and made the choice to grow. We had to persevere for our teammates and our families. And while all of these trials came with plenty of failure and doubt, our willingness to adapt and grow ultimately saw us through and provided us with the resolve and confidence that fuels us to this day.

That kind of growth is waiting for us all on the other side of adversity, and perseverance can get us there. If you're in the midst of a particularly brutal period, that growth is what you and your teammates need right now. We know because it's what we all need. And you'll lead them through that growth by modeling it, because confidence is contagious.

The world will only get faster paced and complex as time goes on. We need wiser leaders. We need disciplined leaders. We need purposeful leaders. We need confident leaders. And the real gem hidden within growth is earned confidence, which enables us to lead through the complex and novel problems on the horizon. Persevering leaders take this brand of confidence with them; aware that they cannot predict an uncertain future, they are nonetheless prepared to face it.

EARNED CONFIDENCE

Confidence is hard to come by and must be earned over time. And not all confidence is the same. There is a progression to confidence that cannot be learned or fully experienced in the classroom. Each stage of confidence enables the next, eventually culminating at earned confidence—the external expression of wisdom. *Earned confidence* is a special combination of preparation and experience, developed and honed through many iterations of execution and reflection.

We can't get earned confidence from books or podcasts or fake it until we make it. We have to get some reps. We have to build confidence through the stages of base confidence and learned confidence to grow earned confidence. The Army has a great way of developing this by applying the crawl-walk-run approach to all training. When you see a video of some barrel-chested freedom fighters blowing doors off their hinges and clearing buildings, you can rest assured that it took a lot of reps in the arena to get there.

Close Quarters Battle (CQB)—that is, fighting in urban terrain—is a great illustration of progressing through the stages of confidence. It is the most exciting, most dangerous, and by far the most addictive aspect of being a Special Operator. When done with precision, it's a terrifying and effective dance of chaos and order. Those who have experienced it can attest there is nothing quite like it. But CQB competence doesn't just happen overnight. In fact, the first time through the shoot house is always awkward and ugly; plus, well before that, there's a long road to earning the shoot house. You don't get through the door of the shoot house until you're ready. You don't get to shoot live rounds two feet off your buddy's barrel unless you're confident.

First you must learn how to use your weapon effectively and safely. You must qualify with your weapon; get through the flat range; learn how to load, fire, and clear jams; put rounds where you want them; put rounds where you want them while moving; and then tighten up your shot group. When you've learned how to do all of that without pointing the barrel of your weapon at your teammate, then you can progress.

And that's just individual training. Then, you must learn CQB's tactics, techniques, and procedures: the formations, expectations, signals, commands, and so on. You do that during tape drills,* in open areas with empty weapons. Then, you do flow drills in buildings before you work up to the shoot house. These steps establish a base level of knowledge, leading to *base confidence*—a general understanding and

---

* Modeling a room or floor plan on the ground with white engineer tape and then doing CQB "flow drills" so that everyone can observe, review, and learn.

familiarity with what is expected of operators to be successful. That base is then ready to be tested in the shoot house.

Entering the shoot house for the first time is like a first kiss. You generally know what to expect and approach it eagerly, but you never understand the feeling until go time. In CQB, all the base knowledge comes together when you feel the heat of the door charge on your face, the taste of dust and carbon in your mouth, or the crunch of bullet casings under your boots. It's scary and exhilarating all at once.

The fast pace is disorienting at first. You can enter the same shoot house a thousand times and feel like you're walking into a thousand different rooms. In and out of the stack you go—assault, clear, secure, extract, review, and repeat. Execute, reflect, learn, refine, execute. Over and over. Day after day until the lights go out, and you do it again night after night—until you understand. You understand the feeling of your heart in your ears and the blast of the charge on your palate. You understand the pinch in your forearm from operating your weapon one-handed while working with your free hand. You understand the feeling of live rounds zinging past your head, and the focus that comes with it.

Time under tension in the shoot house changes you until you have the learned confidence to step into the real arena: combat. Championships aren't won on the practice field. We play the game because we can't simply forecast the score using previous records and rosters. The price of admission into the arena is *learned confidence*—knowing that you can successfully perform a task under certain conditions because you've done it many times.

The thing about learned confidence is that it's close to earned confidence, but they are not the same. True mastery can only be earned in the arena, in real life, at game speed. *Earned confidence* allows us to consistently and expertly apply our skills and experience to familiar endeavors, but more importantly, it allows us to take all of our preparation and experience and apply it to new or unfamiliar challenges.

Kicking down doors in a foreign land is different from blowing through the shoot house. Similar but different. A certain amount of muscle memory moves you forward, but the feeling is not at all the same. The stakes are much higher, and as much as you'd like to pretend it's just another target, you know that it's not. All sorts of weird and unpredictable things happen. You get dropped off in the wrong spot, a barking dog blows your security, somebody trips going through the door, the dust is so thick you can hardly see, women and children are in the building, you name it. Regardless of how it's portrayed in the movies, these kinds of operations very rarely, if ever, go according to plan.

Real-life decisions, with real-life consequences, occur in real time in the arena. And we cannot lead in that environment by rigidly following a checklist or flowchart. We have to deeply understand the principles of our work, execute with great skill, and most importantly, demonstrate the judgment to adapt on the fly. Because while we can reflect and refine during after-action reviews, we cannot take anything back. Once we pull the trigger, we cannot put that round back in the chamber.

Earned confidence cannot be faked. It accrues through the losses and the wins in the arena, where the losses are equally as valuable as the wins, if not more so. The losses force us to learn and to decide if, when, and how we go back into the arena. Mistakes and failures require us to decide whether we'll give in to doubt and discouragement, or whether we'll grow and allow ourselves to be changed. That's where wisdom waits, and it takes place every day around us and inside of us.

When we consistently decide to persevere and reenter the arena, we develop an earned confidence that can never be taken from us. It remains with us even as we enter new arenas of competition—like leaving service and starting a career in the civilian sector, leaving one industry to begin in another, or wiping the slate clean after a great year to set our sights on the year ahead. Every endeavor offers us a new arena to step forward with the earned confidence we gained from our experience. This is so important because every adversity is a new arena in itself, and no two are the same—similar, yes, but not the same.

Consider the leaders that we spoke about in this book's introduction. MZ, JL, and TA were all accomplished leaders who entered a new arena with new forms of adversity. We trust many of you can relate. You may be staring at a round of layoffs in your company. You may have lost a key player on the team to another opportunity and are scrambling to fill the void. Maybe you are leaving the company you've grown up in for 20 years to challenge yourself in a new opportunity. Whether it's starting a new business or having a new baby, we need to remember that nothing worth having is easy. And while we may not have experienced this particular brand of adversity before, we can go forward with a sense of earned confidence, gained from having persevered through previous adversity. Though we all have much to learn, we are certainly wiser today than we were before. With this growth, we can now approach future challenges proactively, playing to win rather than merely playing not to lose.

PLAYING TO WIN

Playing to win and playing not to lose differ massively. When we play to win, we focus on the task at hand, concern ourselves with what is within our control, and stay on the attack. When we start playing not to lose, we tighten up, hoping to hang on to what we have and defending against a negative outcome. We start worrying about things outside of our control and become reactive.

We've all caught ourselves playing not to lose at some point. It typically happens when we find ourselves in uncharted territory, perhaps feeling a bit of imposter syndrome. We suddenly worry that maybe we're out of our depth and we'll soon be exposed. Or maybe we're thinking that things have gone too well for too long, and we start waiting for the other shoe to drop. This is especially prevalent in competitive sports.

We've all witnessed an underdog go into halftime with an unexpected lead. No doubt, they've earned that lead. They came out in the first half and executed beautifully. They played well and deserved to be ahead as they went into the locker room. Then the energy shifts. The team takes a breath, looks around, and starts to think, *Holy shit, we're winning!*—and the momentum is already going the other way. The team comes out for the second half, and rather than trying to extend their lead, they try to defend it. At some point, they get a bad break, or their opponent makes a great play, and before you know it, the lead has disappeared and the game slips away. What they should have done was continue playing to win. They should have used their lead as evidence that they were the better team that day and come out of the locker room attacking, trying to extend their lead and bury the other team's hopes. The great irony of playing not to lose is that it almost guarantees that you will, in fact, lose.

Playing not to lose is, more than anything, a failure to embrace growth. When we fail to recognize the clear evidence that we can perform at a high level or push through adversity, we miss the opportunity to seize the confidence that we've earned. Growth isn't simply acknowledging where we need to improve, it is wholeheartedly accepting where we are excellent. What is the point of all the struggle and stress and suffering if we don't emerge on the other side feeling more capable and confident? If we are going to play, we might as well play to win.

9

Go Together

BLAYNE SMITH AND BRANDON YOUNG

> If you want to go fast, go alone. If you want to go
> far, go together.
> —*Native American proverb*

This book opened with a few stories about young Army leaders struggling to persevere and guide teams through brutal circumstances in Afghanistan. Throughout the book, we offered numerous anecdotes about how the Special Operations community works to build and test perseverance. And while these stories are instructive, illustrating the nature of leading through uncertainty, they are far from complete.

Our greatest lessons in perseverance occurred outside of the uniform and the structure the Army afforded us. While we appreciate the foundation the Army provided, life outside the military proved far more uncertain for us and (we imagine) is far more relatable for you. We'd love to tell you that we seamlessly transitioned all of our skills and experiences and immediately started crushing life after leaving the military, but that wouldn't be true. We struggled. And we had to learn how to persevere again.

Life in the Army wasn't easy, but it was simple. We were assigned units to lead and missions to accomplish. We knew where we needed to be and what we needed to do. And sometimes, people were trying to kill us, which made us very motivated to get up in the morning and do our very best. Army life also focused our teammates in ways that did not require much additional leadership effort. In these ways, the military tried to create a sense of certainty in an otherwise uncertain world. Life in the "real world" is not like this at all. The real world does not dictate the nature of our lives and relationships, nor does it prescribe a protocol for how we should manage them.

The primary driver of perseverance in the military is not achievement or money. It's the person who stands to our left and to our right. As hokey as it may sound, our brothers and sisters in arms truly motivate us more than anything else. We are committed to protecting them when we are strong, and they are there to support us when we are weak. As the Army often reminds us, it's "mission first, people always." Through all the peaks and valleys, the people were always the point.

Then, one day (for both of us), that team, those relationships, and that very obvious and powerful sense of purpose were gone. And there we were, a couple of big, tough men—with years of experience successfully leading teams in some of the world's most challenging conditions—completely lost. We had uniforms full of badges and tabs in our closets that we couldn't put back on and wouldn't have meant much to anybody if we had. We had skills and attributes that had served us well in combat but weren't particularly well suited for life at home. We had friends aplenty, but they were all off fighting the war while we struggled to be friendly with our families.

SO MUCH FOR THE AFTERGLOW

When you're a barrel-chested freedom fighter who has successfully led in combat and faced down the enemies of our country, it can be easy to feel 10 feet tall and unbeatable. Sometimes, it can feel like we can intimidate life! We do hard things, thinking we're persevering, when in fact we're actually enduring. When you master endurance, you can keep running no matter what life throws at you. But life cannot be intimidated or outrun. We knew how to endure and how to suffer, and that is an acceptable way to get through Ranger School or Special Forces Selection, but it's a crappy way to live a whole life. Within a couple of years after leaving the Army, we both faced the consequences of enduring through adversity when the situations required perseverance. Blayne's story went like this.

————

I spent much of my first two years out of the Army in a deep valley. I had lost my sense of purpose. I missed my teammates. And I was ashamed of how my military career had ended. For almost nine years, I was at the very top of my peer group, assigned to the best units and the toughest missions. Then, on my last deployment, it all came crashing down. In my estimation, I had gotten five of my friends killed, was blown out of a firebase, and limped through the rest of the trip; then I quit. Sadly, I didn't have the awareness or the tools to understand and process that kind of trauma, so I just decided to put my head down and work . . . to just keep pushing. That was a bad approach, not only for me but also my whole family.

Something that I'd failed to appreciate was how much my deployment had affected everybody. My then-wife was home, pregnant with Dalton, while reports came in about our friends being killed and wounded. I shudder when I imagine what it must have been like trying to parent a precocious three-year-old, navigate a high-risk pregnancy, and console a group of grieving widows, all while living in constant fear that the next knock on the door could be to inform you that your husband is dead.

This is where our strength became a weakness and eventually ended our marriage. I came home with all ten fingers and toes and felt damn lucky to have done so. I landed a good job, bought a nice home, and had two beautiful little boys. In my mind, I had nothing to complain about. I believe that my wife felt very similarly about her situation. Regardless of what it looked like from the outside, however, we were not well. We both felt like we could gut it out and see our respective ways out of the valley, and so we just went on suffering quietly, separately. Then, in a blink, it was over.

In the wake of our separation and ultimate divorce, I sought professional support for my mental health and was able to see things much more clearly. I left my corporate job and took a role leading a small nonprofit organization called Team RWB. I rented a great little house on Davis Island, near downtown Tampa, and was starting to make friends. Life was looking up, but being a single dad is no easy task. I certainly tried my best to be there for the boys, but I was still going 1,000 miles per hour. I was leading a startup organization with big dreams and trying to carve out a new life for myself. The boys were troopers, and we had a lot of fun, but they mostly lived on my terms. I dragged them to a million Team RWB events, rushed them off to bed when I had evening conference calls, and had a before-school prelaunch sequence that would put a NASCAR pit crew to shame. Raising two little boys had my fully *divided* attention. Then I found Jeni.

Meeting Jeni and later having Penny felt like such an amazing opportunity; it was an elusive second bite at the apple. One of life's rare second chances to do things right—to be the husband and dad that I had always wanted to be but hadn't always been. As my life started to come into focus, I didn't always like what I saw, but I was grateful to be seeing more clearly. Jeni's influence was huge. She provided a ton of encouragement and support for my role at Team RWB, but also really helped me to understand how the boys needed me. We talked a lot about building a life that would take some emphasis off of work and place more on our family. And for a while, we pulled it off fairly well.

By the end of 2016, we were living what I'd call a truly integrated life. Though it was far from perfect (or easy), we'd settled into a life that felt full and sustainable. Our careers allowed us to earn a living doing work we cared about. We had a lovely home in a nice neighborhood. The kids were in a rhythm, and we had an awesome community of friends. Things were solid and steady, right up until I couldn't take it anymore. Solid and steady began to feel stagnant and slow. The ambition monster was in my ear.

What are we gonna do next? Where do we go from here? How can we keep progressing? Surely, we can't run this nonprofit forever. On and on it went. It was all just too comfortable. I was starting to fall off the pace! I had to step it up, make a move, and find another mountain to climb. That mountain presented itself as an opportunity to move to Jacksonville Beach and become the president of one of my favorite companies, GORUCK.

We knew that moving four hours away would be a huge shift in the family dynamics, and Jeni and I mulled it over endlessly. Ultimately, we decided that we could make it work. We'd have less time with the boys, but we'd make sure to focus on quality and maximize our time during holidays and over the summer. Maybe having one clear, primary home with their mom would be easier for them. We sold our house, packed our stuff, and left Tampa behind. It was an exciting move, and life was immediately great at the beach, but it only took a few months and a couple dozen long drives to realize that we'd left behind much more than our hometown.

We could feel the boys pulling away. All the hours in the car, the missed moments, and the disruptions in their lives were taking a toll. We still had fun when we were together, but you could feel our relationships fundamentally changing and becoming more transactional. There was no more homework or packing lunches or soccer practice. They didn't live with us anymore; they were just visiting. The distance just kept getting greater, and they eventually stopped returning most of my messages and rarely answered a FaceTime request. It was a painful reality to confront.

I had been here before in so many ways. I was running hard at another summit with half of my family on the climb and the other half in the valley. Jeni and I knew we couldn't continue at this pace and decided to return to Tampa. I left my dream job at GORUCK with no plan other than to return home. The uncertainty of what was to come troubled me deeply. I felt torn, in desperate need of a deep, emotional wake-up call. Little did I know, I had one coming.

Our time in Jacksonville Beach was coming to a close. Jeni was starting to spend a lot of time back in Tampa, ramping up her new job, and I got to be with Penny a ton more. Sometimes, it was just her and me for four or five days. I felt like I was mostly doing a pretty good job of being her dad, but my head was often elsewhere. I was consumed with thoughts and concerns about what we'd do next. *Should we buy a house? Where will I work? Are people disappointed in me?* On and on.

Through it all, Penny was a good friend. We went to breakfast together, played at the beach, and covered countless miles in her jogging stroller and bike seat. One beautiful spring evening, Penny and I were strolling about Neptune Beach. It was the kind of night that reminds you why you love living in Florida. Warm but not hot. The sky was a perfect cornflower blue, and a little breeze was blowing in off the ocean. The sidewalks were alive with a light sort of energy that you get in beach towns. On this particular night, we were doing our favorite activity—eating frozen custard from Whit's.

So there we were, walking back to our bike, a sugary smile on Penny's curious and charming face as she continued what we called her "campaign for Mayor of Neptune Beach." She waved in all the restaurant windows, jabbered with people on the sidewalk, and picked up every single piece of trash in sight. It was a nice night, and I was in a good mood, but almost instinctively, I started to hurry her along.

We didn't have anywhere to be. Nobody was waiting for us. Yet the words just rolled off my tongue like they had a thousand times before: "Come on, sweetie, we need to get going."

Suddenly, I heard a man's voice calling from behind me: "Sir! Sir!" I turned around to see if he was talking to me and noticed a homeless man sitting on a bench. My instinctive reaction was avoidance. I figured if I didn't make eye contact, we could just keep moving along, but it was too late. He looked right at me and again said, "Sir!" Reluctantly, I answered him with a "Hey."

"You should learn to enjoy going at her pace."

I was caught completely off guard. His words cut through the clutter in my mind—the self-doubt, the questions, the predictions, and the fear. With ringing clarity, the words woke me from my stupor.

"You should learn to enjoy going at her pace."

You see, I had always lived life at *my* pace. *I* pushed the pace. I was relentless in my pursuit of the things that mattered to me. Personality profiles often describe me as an Achiever and Arranger, which can be a highly productive but dangerous combination. Being obsessed with both accomplishment and efficiency is great for getting shit done. That part seems quite obvious. Less obvious were all the things I was missing and all the damage I was doing while doggedly chasing down accomplishment after accomplishment. From life's simple joys to some pretty significant warning signs, my drive to do more often blinded me to things that were truly important.

I was a pro at writing off my personal agenda as serving the greater good. After all, who else was going to provide for my family, save us all from terrorism, and rebuild the American dream?! It had to be me, right? The hard truth is that most of my pursuits had been pretty selfish. And while my desire to "fulfill my potential" has certainly done some good, it's often left those closest and most important to me feeling like role players in my life—which is a huge problem, because they *are* my life.

My oldest son Dylan's life had been at my pace. He was born when I was in the Special Forces Qualification Course. When he was one week old, I had to go to Washington, DC, for a week of training. When he was six weeks old, I left for another five weeks of training. And on it went. By the time I got home from Afghanistan in 2009, he was more than three years old, and I'd been away for more than half his life.

Dalton was born just a couple of weeks after I got back from that deployment, and he didn't fare much better. While I was there physically, my mind was mostly just ping-ponging between the recent past and the near future. I was alternately consumed with the grief and guilt of losing five teammates a few months earlier in Afghanistan and figuring out what I was going to do with my life as I exited the Army just a little later that year.

And then it just got harder. By Dalton's third birthday, his mother and I were divorced, unable to collectively and harmoniously navigate our post-military transition. It's a long and complicated story, as most divorces are, but if I had to attribute our marriage's failure to one thing, it would be this: we were all trying to endure our new life with the tools that got us through our Army life, but the situation had changed, and we failed to change with it and persevere together.

No more.

Now, change was upon us. The ridgeline of my life was renewed, and Jeni and I chose to grow together. We chose to go home together.

The decision to head back to Tampa was a difficult one, but the right one. We'd created a lot of chaos for ourselves and at least a little for others. It felt shitty. I was worried. My brain was spinning. And then a homeless man made it all very simple for me. My whole life in one sentence.

"You should *learn* to *enjoy* going *at her pace.*"

He didn't say that I should go at her pace. He didn't say that I should enjoy going at her pace. He said that I should learn to enjoy going at her pace. It hit me like a damn bolt of lightning. I had rarely ever gone at anybody else's pace, and if I had, I probably didn't enjoy it. I wasn't even sure what that would feel like. My mind just kept flashing to the countless times that I'd shooed the kids along or rushed off to the office or said, "Not today, honey," when I could have easily said, "Sure, why not?" It made me feel sick to my stomach. I really did have a lot to learn. Fortunately, our little Penny was a great teacher.

Slowly but surely, I adjusted my pace, and though it felt unnatural, I began to enjoy it. It's amazing all of the little things you notice by following around a curious toddler. Seeing the world through her eyes made it seem so much richer and more exciting. I started catching myself saying "Wow!" more than Owen Wilson in a buddy movie.

And here's the best part: I still felt motivated to work and contribute professionally. Slowing down and going at her pace didn't turn me into some kind of lazy freeloader. In fact, it gave me the time and space to think hard and do good work. Most importantly, it allowed me to walk down life's path together with the whole family.

The hardest part for me was all about identity. I went from being a Green Beret to the CEO of Team RWB to the president of

GORUCK, and now, who would I be? Just some guy? It seems a little silly now, but that question bothered me. Penny showed me that it was okay to start with being "Penny's dad" and take it from there.

Going at her pace taught me that the best things in life are meant to be shared. It helped me to realize that while being alone in the valley is obviously bad, it is not much better to be alone at the summit—you're still alone. And it taught me that sometimes, our best training, capabilities, and willingness to endure hardship reach the extent of their usefulness. Sometimes, the grittiest and gutsiest thing you can do is surrender and change. It is in those times when we need our people the most so that we may grow and go together.

———

By now, it might not surprise you that Brandon's story is oddly similar. His post-Army experience went like this.

———

I left the Army in 2009 to be a husband and a dad. I had spent most of our eight-year marriage deployed or preparing to deploy and knew our family couldn't sustain the pace any longer. I felt ashamed of being an absent father and knew the kids deserved better—a realization that struck the day I saw Elliot born into the world. It remains the most amazing experience of my life. Eager to achieve in a new profession, I took a sales job that put me in a hotel three nights a week, driving 60,000 miles a year around my expansion territory. My hopes for a better future for our family and my actions only mildly matched up, adding more stress to our fragile marriage.

The time was difficult for our family, and I forcefully made all the justifications for my absence: "I got paid peanuts in the Army, and now we get our payday." "I'm providing for our family!" "At least I'm not deployed for six months." "We're racking up hotel points, babe!" The truth is, I did what I knew to do best—I put my head down and ran. I ran at the next achievement. I ran away from my family. And I ran from being a sales professional. Oh, sure, I logged my calls and did the moves, but it was enough for me to feel liked by someone instead of being effective for my company, and I failed to achieve my number two years running.

Eighteen months after leaving the Army, I even tried to run back to the war through a three-letter government agency. It was easier for me to return to war than to my family. But that wasn't the path for me. With little notice and for no apparent reason, that door was slammed in my face. Within weeks, my company offered to transfer me to Colorado for a fresh start in a viable territory. Kelly and I agreed over a 30-second phone call; we left Georgia 30 days later. In many ways, it felt like a freedom bird extracting us from a dark valley of heartbreak.

Colorado offered a chance for a better future, but we can't snap our fingers and make everything better. It takes time, effort, and support. *I* needed help. At work, I had mentors and leaders who invested in me and challenged me. I also had a "cut the crap" moment with myself and committed to giving sales one more year, but the right way. I was going to do the hard work instead of the moves—the real effort required to win, not just the activities that looked good on paper—and it worked. Still, even as I started winning professionally, I felt alone every day, separated from my Ranger family and the family Kelly and I had created. *We* needed help.

Year after year, I wrestled with memories from the past and couldn't shake this gnawing question: *Why is it that whenever I was about to die in the war, I was crying out to God for help, but I never acknowledge him otherwise?* "Why?" can be a bottomless question but also a light in the darkness. I was seeking. I read the Psalms, philosophy, and the social sciences; joined men's groups; read books; and challenged people to explain what they knew to be "truth." Kelly was seeking too. And we both noticed Jaden struggling in school and friendships. Grasping for a way to help him, Kelly mentioned that her mom encouraged her to pray when she was scared and frequently reminded Kelly to "Let go and let God." But we had no frame to operate from, so we kept seeking. Separately.

Some friends at the gym invited us to come to their church, and Kelly agreed. One Sunday morning, we rolled into the parking lot of what looked like a mega-mall. My facial expression undoubtedly prompted Kelly's immediate apology: "I'm so sorry." We were overwhelmed, but we had committed, so we put our heads down and pressed on . . . right into the lobby where a kind man extended his hand and said, "Welcome, glad you're here," with no trace of guile or sarcasm.

Week after week, we came back. Week after week, that kind man with the white hair and a warm smile said, "Hey!" He got to know us, and we looked forward to seeing him. And the pastor spoke in a way I had never heard from a Christian authority figure. He faced the hard parts of the Bible, offered differing perspectives of the text, walked with us through the nuance, and treated us like we were smart. And I could hear what he was saying without the need to argue. It was like those long nights in the Georgia backwoods training for Best Ranger with Jeremiah when we talked about God, life, and our families. And something unexpected happened.

I had predicted all the wreckage and the inevitable outcomes. I could see it all coming—the anger, the war, the trauma, the sadness, the contempt, and the divorce—it all made sense to me. I couldn't see Jesus coming. I couldn't see myself surrendering. But I did. And while I'd love to tell you everything was rainbows and Ferris wheels after that; it wasn't. That's not the way it works. God is not a slot machine. There are no silver bullets in life, no elevators to the summit. There is truth, love, and effort—seeking in earnest, yet imperfect. And that's what we did. We sought God's best for us, not our best for ourselves, even as that hardwiring to run still burned inside of me.

I'd won in sales, earned a team, and made a lot of money, and by all accounts, everything looked great on the outside because I was a pro at managing my reputation. But on the home front, a chasm remained between my family and me. I felt the call to do something for military people, and out of the blue, I received a call one day from Blayne. He had left our company 18 months before to lead a veteran nonprofit called Team RWB and asked if I'd join him to help generate revenue for the mission. I left my corporate job and took a 60% pay cut the same month Kelly got accepted to nursing school. God provided, and we made it work. And I ran hard at the mission—all the way to Portland, Los Angeles, Bentonville, New York, Seattle, San Francisco, and everywhere in between. I had a mission! America's veterans needed me. *I* needed to help *them*. Or so I thought.

After a few years at Team RWB and many veteran interactions, I walked back into the Veterans Affairs and started over. My shipmate,[*] Dana, made me. She was aghast when I told her I had no healthcare support from the VA and said, "I'm going to introduce you to a friend. He's a Marine and a veteran advocate. Please just meet with him and try to keep an open mind." I sat with him. I listened, and I talked. And though I didn't think I needed the VA's help, something he said clicked: "Brother, the way you're living life isn't normal. But don't take it from me. Take it from your wife."

He sent me home with an assignment—two copies of a worksheet with an image of a knight and various statements written next to pieces of its armor and weapons. The statements were behavioral observations, like rage (for the sword), hypervigilance (for the shield), trouble sleeping (for the helmet), and many others. Kelly and I were instructed to complete the assignments alone and seal them in two manila envelopes. We circled the behaviors we observed in me, sealed our envelopes, and returned them the following week. I circled four. Kelly circled all but two. I couldn't unsee the difference. I resubmitted my medical records to the VA in 2015—*all* of them this time—and told the truth in my examinations.

In 2015, I was diagnosed with PTSD, traumatic brain injuries, several musculoskeletal injuries, and nerve damage. I remember weeping in the psychiatrist's examination and hearing her kindly say, "Brandon, you were a Ranger for nine years. You went to war four times . . . did you *really* think it would be any different?" I didn't. But I thought *I* was different. I thought I could out-suffer, out-fight,

_____

* Navy term of endearment.

out-Ranger, or outrun anything and anyone. And in many ways, I could. But in every way, I ended up in the same place: alone.

Three weeks later, I ran the Mt. Evans Ascent with 20 Team RWB members. The Mt. Evans Ascent is America's highest road race, beginning at Echo Lake (10,600 feet of elevation) and running 14.5 miles to the Mt. Evans summit at 14,265 feet. I stood at the starting line with Old Glory on my shoulder and my Winter Strike–issued beanie on my head. Just another day. Just another mountain. Just another challenge. America's veterans *needed* me. Let's go.

I set out fast, like any other run, as the sprawling Rocky Mountain vistas opened up with every bend in the road. The miles dropped while the elevation stacked up, and I drowned out the pain with ear-thumping beats. I can take it. I've been here before.

I'd pass runner after runner, receiving meek greetings from winded athletes.

"Woo!"

"Eagle Up!"

"Yeah!"

"America!"

"All right!"

I'd raise the flag each time and say, "You got this!"

I got this.

Step by step. Up the mountain. It will all be over eventually. Just keep going. Think about your brothers who can't be out here doing this and drive on.

Ten miles in, the beats were getting drowned out by my thoughts—the music became noise, the earbuds irritations. I popped them out and listened to my steady footfalls on the concrete. I looked over the edge to see a crystal alpine lake far in the valley below and wondered how the water would feel on my burning calves. And I thought about it all—the long ruck marches, the sleepless nights, the starving days, and the relentless cold. It seemed like the cold defined my entire Army career.

I thought about all the fights—in school, in the ring, in Afghanistan, in my home. I thought about driving the bodies of the Task Force men killed in an MH-60 crash to the bird at Bagram in 2002. I had fought back tears as I drove the HMMWV through the cordon of saluting teammates. I thought of Dave McDowell's body lying in the open casket at his funeral in 2008—there but somehow, not. Looking down at the waxy, lifeless figure in the box made me hope it wasn't really Dave. That my larger-than-life friend was just waiting to pop out and say, "Gotcha!" But it was Dave's body. He was gone.

And I thought about the visit with the VA psych just weeks before.

"So, you have PTSD," she said.

"That's it?" I asked.

"That's it."

"Let me guess . . . now's the part where you throw me a bag of pills, right?"

"Nope. My prescription for you is yoga. Let's start there, okay?"

"Okay," I said. "Okay."

I replayed the conversation over and over again in my mind. *I have PTSD*. It was oddly freeing to acknowledge it—orienting and clarifying. I had something to hold on to. There was a reason and a way forward. And I wondered how different our family life could be if I could stop the rage, the yelling, the viciousness, and the havoc.

Two miles from the finish line with my three-hour goal well within reach, another thought entered my mind.

I don't want to run anymore.

It wasn't the first time I'd thought this. I remember wishing on some of those long ruck marches that I would break my leg so they'd have to put me in the aid van. But it never happened, and I just kept going. Sometimes, the blood would seep from the drain holes in my boots. One time, I tore all the skin off both pads of my feet. But I kept going. No, it wasn't the first time I'd had this thought. But it was the first time I listened.

I stopped running.

And I started walking.

A runner passed me, and I smiled.

Another came by and said, "Almost there!"

"Yep!" I said.

Another passed, saying, "Man, you've been carrying me up this hill the whole way with that flag. Way to go!"

My smile widened, and I gave him a huge thumbs-up. "*We* got this!" I said.

Another came beside me and said, "You can do this!"

"I know I can," I said. And I kept walking.

Up the mountain I went. One steady foot in front of the other. No drowning beats. No punishing pain. And no surrender to my objective. I adjusted how I got there, not where I got. When I crossed the finish line at 3:02, I felt a joy of accomplishment that had been missing on so many other races or rucks I had previously smashed. I stood at the finish line with the flag, high-fiving finishers and looking out for my teammates. I backtracked the course, found friends making the final push, and cheered them on. And as they ran to the finish line, I just kept walking.

I stopped running, and I started growing.

Three years later, our dear friend Rick (that welcoming man at church with the white hair) and my mentor, Will, officiated and stood with me as we watched Kelly walk down the aisle of our church, Jaden on one side, Elli on the other. We reclaimed what was to have been our original wedding date, remarrying on December 22, 2018, in that big old church that feels oh so small to us. In the years since, we've persevered through the May 7, 2019, STEM Highlands Ranch shooting that ripped our children's school apart; Kelly serving on the front lines of COVID-19 as an ER nurse; serving in marriage minis-try; grad school; and all the other things life has thrown our way. But most importantly, we did it all together. We do it all together.

WIN TOGETHER

This is the final lesson on perseverance. Regardless of what summit we aim for or what path we take, it's better to go together. No achieve-ment is worth destroying relationships or leaving behind the ones we love. And there is no adversity through which we cannot persevere when we have the support of our teammates, friends, and family. That is really why we wrote this book. Yes, we wrote it for you, but *we also wrote it for us*. As you've just read, losing our way along the path is easy, so this concept requires regular reminding.

High-drive, high-achieving people have a very common response to adversity: square up and grind it out. We're willing to take the pain until we get to the other side. The problem is that when we do that, we are likely to leave others behind or create a lot of collateral damage, because life's most important challenges don't require us to simply muscle through them. They require us to adapt and grow—together.

As we've said throughout the book, there are certainly times when the right answer is to suck it up and gut it out. But we can't do that forever, and we can't do that alone. Endurance is a wonderful tactic to help us survive, but perseverance allows us to *thrive*—and that is what we wish for you.

PHOTOS

October 2001: Brandon Young in Jordan at sunrise during a training mission with Alpha Company (A Co.) 2/75 Ranger Regiment. PHOTO BY JUSTIN VIENE

October 2001: Brandon Young and members of 2nd PLT A Co. 2/75 Ranger, "The Blacksheep," fast-roping during training in Jordan. PHOTO BY JUSTIN VIENE

2003: The Madslashers, 1st PLT Charlie Company (C Co.) 2/75 Ranger Regiment, Asadabad, Kunar Province, Afghanistan.

2003: Brandon, Kelly, and Jaden Young at the McChord Air Force Base Troop Holding Area after Brandon returned from an Afghanistan rotation.

2003: Elements of the 1st and 2nd Ranger Battalions load vehicles for the ground insertion up the Pech Valley; FOB Catamount (later renamed FOB Blessing), Nangalam, Afghanistan.

2003: 1st Platoon (Madslashers) C Co. 2/75 Ranger Regiment, Kantiwa South, Nuristan Province, Afghanistan, Winter Strike.

2003: Winter Strike Kantiwa South, Nuristan Province, Afghanistan;
Brandon, Jon W., Jeff, and Jon.

SGT Jay Anthony Blessing,
KIA November 14, 2003,
Nangalam, Afghanistan.*

2006: Brandon Young competing in the
Best Ranger Competition. PHOTO BY ABBY
PITTMAN

* The appearance of U.S. Department of Defense (DoD) visual information does
not imply or constitute DoD endorsement.

2006: Brandon Young and Jeremiah Pittman, Best Ranger Competition finish (third place). PHOTO BY ABBY PITTMAN

2006: Brandon Young with his daughter, Elliot, saying good-bye to the 75th Ranger Regiment.

SFC David L. McDowell, KIA April 29, 2008, Bastion, Afghanistan.*

2009: Blayne Smith in Uruzgan Province, Afghanistan.

2009: View of Khas Uruzgan Valley looking south from Firebase Anaconda.

2009: Blayne Smith with Afghan children near Firebase Anaconda.

2009: Dave Hurt and Blayne Smith outside the Khas Uruzgan police station near Firebase Anaconda.

2009: SSG Marc Small near Firebase Anaconda. KIA February 12, 2009, Faramuz, Afghanistan.

2009: SSgt. Tim Davis, USAF, near Firebase Anaconda. KIA February 20, 2009, Khas Uruzgan, Afghanistan.

2009: ODA 3123 and their Czech Special Forces counterparts just before departing Firebase Anaconda.

2009: Dave Hurt, Marc Small, and Jeremy Bessa on a rooftop at Firebase Anaconda. MSG Dave Hurt and SSG Jeremy Bessa KIA February 20, 2009, Khas Uruzgan, Afghanistan.

2009: Firebase Anaconda.

2009: Blayne on a rooftop in northern Helmand just a few minutes before the Taliban attacked the position.

2009: Blayne in northern Helmand Province as the team prepares to board extraction helicopters.

2015: The Mt. Evans Ascent; Brandon on its summit.

2018: Blayne Smith receiving the inaugural Military Service Citation from the George W. Bush Institute.

2018: The Youngs.

2018: The Smiths.

2020: Blayne Smith, costarring in *The Standard*, on Amazon Prime, Apple TV, and Hulu.

2020: Blayne and Penny in the spring.

ACKNOWLEDGMENTS

We would like to acknowledge the amazing people who have made this book possible. We have to start with our wonderful families, who have supported us throughout the long journey. Without your love and encouragement, this thing never would have stood a chance of seeing the light of day. Thank you for believing in us and sharing this life with us. We need to thank Matt Holt and the incredible team at Matt Holt/BenBella Books. You've been a dream to work with, and we could not have asked for a better team to have by our side as we navigated the process. Your knowledge, experience, and insight were critical to every step along the way. None of this would have happened without our agent, Greg Johnson, and WordServe Literary betting on us and guiding us through the often confusing and difficult process of writing a proposal and selling a book. Thank you for trusting us and showing us the way! Last, we are so incredibly grateful to the countless friends and partners who have challenged and encouraged us to write a book. To all of those who listened to our ideas, gave us feedback, reviewed our manuscript, and reassured us when we were doubtful, we owe you a beer (or three).

Brandon would like to thank:

God the Father, Jesus Christ, and the Holy Spirit—who give life, sustain life, and renew life—to you be the glory! My wife, Kelly, my love, best friend, and co-adventurer—thank you for challenging me to be a better man every day. Our children, Jaden and Elliot—you have animated my purpose to persevere and taught me forgiveness, love, and joy. You two are incredible—I am proud of you both. My mom (Bonnie), for teaching me how to endure. My brother (Bryan), and my sister (Blythe)—for walking through tough valleys together, and for all the laughter. I love you, your spouses, and your children. Lifelong mentors Michele, Jason, Matt, Joe, and Tara—thank you for modeling authentic leadership and challenging me . . . Big L. My mentor Will—thank you for modeling authentic manhood and for discipling me in the ways of Jesus Christ . . . I love you, pal. Rangers—thank you for showing me how to lead, sacrifice, and persevere; thank you for entrusting me with your lives at times and your hearts at others. Thank you for being my family. I especially want to thank Justin, Jon, Donnie, Tony, and Chris for revisiting Winter Strike with me and confirming accuracy and tone. My incredible mentors at Denver Seminary, Tim, Joey, and Knut—each of you sharpened me and challenged me to bring our work into the world. And, of course, my friend and business partner, Blayne—your keen wit, cool demeanor, and superior grit have changed my life. Thank you! I couldn't have a better partner on this adventure, brother.

Blayne would like to thank:

My wonderful wife, Jeni, for believing in me, challenging me, and supporting me through all of life's ups and downs. Your love and friendship sustain me, and your spirit inspires me. Our beautiful kids, Dylan, Dalton, and sweet little Penny. Being your dad is easily the most humbling and most rewarding job I've ever had. I love you all so much! To my parents, who raised me and loved me from the time I was a precocious child to an (often overly) ambitious man—thank you for showing me such unconditional support and for teaching me how to live a meaningful life. To my Army buddies and teammates, I love you and miss you. To Alex, Alex, Jimmy, JJ, and Mac—thanks for helping me cut my teeth as a leader and for introducing me to real music. To Aaron, Billy, Cessa, Todd, and the Darkhorse crew— thanks for trusting me and keeping me safe. To Casey, Gus, Linsey, Eric, and all the boys from ODA 3123—thanks for being there to pick me up, both in combat and well beyond. And finally, I must thank my business partner and dear friend, Brandon, without whom none of this would have been possible. Your passion, enthusiasm, and partnership are incredible blessings, and I'm so proud to be on the trail with you.

NOTES

1. Dwight Eisenhower, "A Speech to the National Defense Executive Reserve Conference in Washington, D.C., November 14, 1957," *Public Papers of the Presidents of the United States, Dwight D. Eisenhower, 1957* (Washington, DC: National Archives and Records Service, Government Printing Office, 1957), 818.
2. Helmut von Moltke, "Military Works: II. Activity as Chief of the Army General Staff in Peacetime, Article on Strategy" (Berlin: Ernst Siegfried Mittler und Sohn, 1871), 291.
3. Kate Murphy, *You're Not Listening: What You're Missing and Why It Matters* (New York: Celadon, 2020), 166.
4. Steve Cuss, *Managing Leadership Anxiety: Yours and Theirs* (Nashville: Thomas Nelson, 2019), 122.
5. Caroline M. Angel et al., "Team Red, White & Blue: A Community-Based Model for Harnessing Positive Social Networks to Enhance Enrichment Outcomes in Military Veterans Reintegrating to Civilian Life," *Translational Behavioral Medicine* 8, no. 4 (2018): 554–64, https://doi.org/10.1093/tbm/iby050.
6. Angel et al., "Team Red, White & Blue."
7. James Stockdale, interview by Jim Collins, *Good to Great: Why Some Companies Make the Leap . . . and Others Don't* (New York: Harper Business, 2001).

8. William Irvine, *A Guide to the Good Life: The Ancient Art of Stoic Joy* (Oxford, UK: Oxford University Press, 2009).

9. Mengxi Dong, Nic M. Weststrate, and Marc A. Fournier, "Thirty Years of Psychological Wisdom Research: What We Know About the Correlates of an Ancient Concept," *Perspectives on Psychological Science* 18, no. 4 (July 2023): 778–811, https://doi.org/10.1177/17456916221114096.

10. Dong et al., "Thirty Years."

11. Pew Research Center, "Internet, Broadband Fact Sheet," updated January 31, 2024, https://www.pewresearch.org/internet/fact-sheet /internet-broadband/.

12. Dong et al., "Thirty Years."

13. Brené Brown, "Dare to Lead List of Values," accessed November 13, 2023, https://brenebrown.com/resources/dare-to-lead-list-of-values/.

14. Simon Sinek, *Start with Why: How Great Leaders Inspire Everyone to Take Action* (New York: Portfolio/Penguin, 2009), 2–5.

ABOUT THE AUTHORS

Jillian Milam, Early Morning Light Studio

Blayne Smith (right) and Brandon Young (left) co-founded Applied Leadership Partners in 2020 to share hard-earned leadership wisdom with leaders guiding teams through growth, change, or adversity. Applied Leadership Partners is a boutique consulting firm that supports leaders in creating tightly knit, high-performing teams through leadership development training, keynotes, and executive advising.

Brandon Young is a former US Army Ranger with four combat rotations to Afghanistan. He has spent more than 25 years building and leading teams in the military, corporate healthcare, and nonprofit sectors. Brandon has built partnerships with some of the world's most iconic brands, including Nike, Walmart, Starbucks, Microsoft, and Amazon. He is the recipient of the Quest Diagnostics

Regional Excellence Award for Commercial Leadership for his work in cancer diagnostics. He's been published in various magazines and peer-reviewed academic journals; assessed, mentored, and trained more than 1,000 Ranger leaders while serving in the 75th Ranger Regiment; and placed third in the 2006 Best Ranger Competition. Brandon lives in Littleton, Colorado, with his wife, Kelly. They have two adult children: Jaden is a Soldier in the US Army and Elliot is a student at the University of Colorado. Brandon holds a master of divinity in leadership from Denver Seminary, and his passions are faith, family, community, and adventures.

Blayne Smith is a West Point graduate and former Army Special Forces officer who has transitioned into a highly effective business and social impact leader. He is a cofounder and principal at Applied Leadership Partners and the director for health and well-being at the George W. Bush Institute. Blayne also serves on the board of the Armed Services Arts Partnership and as an advisory board member of GORUCK. Previously, Blayne was the first executive director of Team Red, White, and Blue, a veterans' nonprofit that has grown into one of the most trusted and effective organizations in the space. During his time in the military, Blayne led combat units in both Iraq and Afghanistan. He is a Draper Leadership Award recipient, the Distinguished Honor Graduate of the Army's Ranger School, and was awarded three Bronze Stars, including one for valor. Blayne holds an MBA from the University of Florida and currently lives in Maine with his wife and three children.